EQUAL PAY MATTERS

EQUAL PAY MATTERS

Closing *the* Wage Gap *to* Achieve Pay Equity

DAVID WEAVER

Bestselling Author *of Pay Matters*

EQUAL PAY MATTERS

Closing the Wage Gap to Achieve Pay Equity

FIRST EDITION

ISBN   978-1-5445-5255-2 *Hardcover*

978-1-5445-5254-5 *Paperback*

978-1-5445-5256-9 *Ebook*

To my family, friends, mentors, colleagues, clients, and students, whose unwavering support fuels my purpose.

Thank you for believing in me and this mission to provide all employees with equal pay for equal work.

CONTENTS

INTRODUCTION

WHY EQUAL PAY MATTERS

It was the closest I ever got to being a rock star. I'd just stepped away from a microphone, and a line of raving fans awaited me. A superstar and I possessed a few differences. I wasn't in a green room backstage but had just stepped from behind a podium. And it wasn't thousands of adoring fans seeking my autograph, but a little more than fifty anxious high-level executives and senior managers with questions. Still, I'd never had such a passionate response to a speaking gig.

I had to give a presentation on the Massachusetts Equal Pay Act, where I not only explained the law but also discussed the fines for violating it. I'd given that same presentation many times to other industries and organizations, but I never had so many people want to speak with me about it afterward. Concern etched on every face signaled internal organizational problems. And soon enough, I understood what was going on.

"I'm so glad you came here to talk today," said the first guy to speak to me. Turns out, he was the marketing manager. "I have a disclosure to make."

"Yes?" Meanwhile, I'm thinking this can't be good! No one ever introduces good news with *I have a disclosure to make.*

"I have four marketing specialists, three males and one female," he said. "They've all been with me for about five years. The three males make significantly more than the female."

"And they have the same job function?" I asked.

He nodded. "Not only that, but the female is consistently the highest performer. Not just the highest; she is outstanding compared to the men."

"So why isn't she paid the same, or even more?" I had a theory why, but I let him explain.

"She didn't negotiate her pay when she started." He confirmed part of my theory. A key factor contributing to the wage disparity is the salary the person negotiated when they were hired.

"OK, I understand that. But she's been with you for five years. Why hasn't she had adequate increases?"

"I don't have an option for that. My organization gives 3.5 to 4 percent annual increases to everybody. There's no way she'll ever get caught up." Bingo! He just confirmed the rest of my hypothesis.

I wasn't surprised when the next manager I spoke with at that organization was in a similar boat, as was the next and the next. They learned from my presentation that Massachusetts now risked imposing serious fines on them if they didn't establish pay equity, yet they felt they had no choice. How were they going to do this when company policy maxes out at a 4 percent annual increase?

"Thank you for sharing this with me," I told each of them. "Now, go share it with the head of HR."

Let me be clear here: None of those managers felt comfortable with the pay disparity going on. None of them believed that women *should* receive less pay than their colleagues. However, the company allowed prospective employees to negotiate aggressively or not because the hiring process did not clearly define salary ranges. As frequently happens, the women had asked for a lower rate than the men had. That set them up to be behind from the get-go. There would be no way, in a company that limits the percentages for increases each year, for them to be paid what their colleagues were getting.

Thankfully, because of the new equity laws, the company could rectify the situation. The next question was, *How do they do that?*

The answer is what this book will cover: How to achieve pay equity without going broke or losing your best employees.

WHY IS PAY EQUITY AN ISSUE?

Perhaps the most obvious answer to the question, *Why is pay equity an issue?* is: It's a matter of human decency to pay people the same amount of money for doing the same job. Frankly, pay equity should be (and is) a common-sense concept for most people. And the consequences of such unfairness run much deeper.

We are all familiar with the stats that prove women—especially women of color—earn less money than men. But it's not just women. All marginalized people tend to be underpaid for doing the same work that men are doing. That adds up to millions of workers in the United States being paid less than they should be, and that adds up to a much farther and wider negative impact.

The consequences businesses face from hiring people

and paying them less than others include higher turnover and lower morale, both of which damage the company's reputation and invite scrutiny of their performance and organizational integrity. Extending beyond the corporate walls, however, we can see how inequity influences society at large. The less people are paid, the less they can invest in their families, which means the less they can invest in their communities. Fewer school supplies, groceries, clothing, and toys are purchased. Restaurants and other service providers miss out on revenue opportunities. And the list just goes on and on.

Meanwhile, the reverse occurs when pay equity is reached. Employees are more loyal and more engaged with their mission and purpose. The business's reputation improves, making it easier to recruit better, more qualified talent. Likewise, stepping beyond the corporation, we see people spreading their wealth among their community, which improves their lives, the lives of their families, and the societies they live in.

HOW DO WE REACH PAY EQUITY?

I wrote this book for HR professionals and business leaders who not only care about achieving fairness in the workplace, but who want to make it happen. Of course, this book will also benefit those with a looming deadline to achieve pay equity because they live in one state that has either already mandated it or is in the process of getting a law for it on the books.

On the following pages, I'll give a little background on the wage gap, discuss current and proposed legislation demanding pay equity, and then go into detail on how to implement it in your organization.

Throughout, I'll provide strategies, solutions, and real-world examples for identifying and addressing any existing pay gaps. You'll come away from this book armed with what you need to know to transform your organization into one with transparent compensation practices and a culture that is in alignment with legislative requirements.

Be prepared for a little hard work though. As you'll see, I'll challenge the misconception that finding pay equity is a simple spreadsheet exercise. Achieving equity is a matter of making a commitment to fairness and taking the action to back up and support that commitment, even when it might seem easier and more pleasant to bury our heads in the sand. I had one CEO tell me he'd rather scratch his eyes with glass than pay people more money. Yes, this presents a challenge, but always remember it is the right action. Equity matters. It matters to the people who make up your workforce; it matters to your organization at large, and it matters to society.

Someone who knows what they're doing can make fulfilling the promise of equity easier. And I'm that someone.

HOW CAN YOU TRUST ME?

For over thirty years now, I've been involved with compensation systems. In 2016, I founded the Compensation & HR Group, which, among other services, conducts pay equity analyses to uncover wage gaps, and we advise on how to close those gaps. We work with between one hundred and 150 organizations a year, which means I can say I've dealt with virtually every kind of pay-related situation you can think of.

Although the companies I've worked with vary in industry and scope, they all share something in common. Heads of HR will say the same thing to me when they ask for an equal pay audit: "I don't think we have an issue. We're just calling you to get an outside perspective."

They say that for a couple of reasons. The first is because they haven't done a deep enough dive to know what's going on for sure. And the second reason is that no one wants to think they're being unfair. No one, especially no one in the human resources field, wants to believe they are the person who would discriminate against their employees.

But, they are. I've worked with organizations of just about any size, from thirty employees to fifteen thousand, and every single one of them had pay equity issues. So for me, it's gotten to when I hear, "We don't think we have a problem," I respond with, "I'm sure you would never intentionally discriminate with pay inequity, but we need to take a critical look and do an audit to know for sure." And of course, every single one of them is shocked and even appalled when my audits discover issues.

Once the initial reaction fades, I have the pleasure of providing hope. My company's mantra is, "We help close the pay gap one project at a time." That's what we do, and we do it well. Frankly, I have a passion for it. While it can seem disheartening to uncover the discrepancies, it's beyond rewarding to know that by bringing them to light, the organizations can fix them. Equity can be achieved.

But working on one pay gap, one project at a time, is a slow process for us. So I wrote this book as a platform to help speed up that process. Because again, equity matters—especially to the people who are not being paid what they're worth.

HOW TO ACHIEVE PAY EQUITY

The following pages will give you a little background on pay equity, so you'll get a feel for how we all got in this mess to begin with. Then I'll cover why it's such a hot-button issue these days: federal and state legislation mandates. After that, we'll get into the nitty-gritty of how to create internal equity, how to communicate about it with your employees, and how to sustain it.

As the old saying goes, "Knowing is half the battle." Once you know you have a problem, you fix it. Take corrective action. Often, I've seen companies think they can gin up some numbers in a spreadsheet and come up with ranges for each job. Unfortunately, it's not that simple to achieve pay equity. You cannot make up numbers. If you do, unless you're extremely lucky, they will be wrong, and you'll have to deal with employee and candidate questions that you just won't be able to answer as a fallout.

Instead, you need a foolproof process. I know that process well; it's what I do repeatedly for the companies I consult. The first step is to determine the market rate for each position in your company. To do that, you'll need up-to-date job descriptions to compare side-by-side with other companies in your industry and geographic location. For step two, you'll build out salary ranges for each job. Then, step three is when you do a pay equity analysis for every single job by looking at all males and females and comparing their pay, their performance, education, training, and seniority.

Saying "three steps" sounds like it's a simple process, but it can be quite complex. Ultimately, the goal of this book is to help you prepare for this process and get the right answers for each of your positions. Hopefully, by the time you make it to the end, you're armed with both the knowledge and the motivation to do what needs to be done in your company for your employees.

Before we dive into the how-to, though, let's get a look at the background to understand why there is a need for equity to begin with.

UNDERSTANDING THE WAGE GAP

Odds are, if you're reading this book, you're concerned about what's going on in your company. Perhaps you suspect you have a wage gap problem or, like the managers in the Introduction, you know you do, but you have no clear idea about what to do about it. Before you attempt to tackle how to fix the issue, it might be a good idea to understand how and why it became one to begin with. That way, in years to come, history will not repeat itself.

This chapter will summarize what the wage gap is and how we got there.

A LEGACY OF INEQUALITY

In a sense, we've always had a wage gap. If we go back in history far enough, we'll find plenty of examples where only men earned wages. But it wasn't until the twentieth century that we saw data that could identify and define a gap. That's when women entered the workforce in ever-growing numbers. They worked in positions aligned with what they did at home, becoming teachers, nurses, clerks, and maids, or were employed in other domestic work. For unknown reasons, those jobs were less valuable than the work their male peers performed, so employers compensated them at lower rates than in other industries. Similarly, people of color and recent immigrants were forced into lower-paying jobs regardless of their skills or intellect. As you'll discover in Chapter 2, where I go into the laws in detail, legislators introduced new laws in the 1920s, post–World War II, and in the 1960s to address inequities among people doing equal work. However, enforcement was always weak and inconsistent, and no one ever thought it was important to officially define what "equal work" meant.

Subsequently, we are where we are today. Granted, blatant discrimination is a thing of the past. However, like gum on the underside of an otherwise clean table at the corner diner, a wage gap remains.

There is one difference between inequity today versus a hundred years ago. While in the early 1900s the wage gap resulted from women and minorities being excluded from better-paying positions, today, in theory, everyone is working in similar capacities. I hope you noticed that "in theory." Because occupational segregation is still a thing. And even when they share job functions with the men around them, they're not paid the same because of systems and structures embedded within organizations. Let's take a deeper look at these variables contributing to wage gaps in today's companies.

KEY FACTORS CONTRIBUTING TO THE GENDER AND RACIAL WAGE GAPS

To reiterate something I said earlier, I have never consulted with a company where anyone thought it was a good idea to pay women and minorities less. No one I've ever worked with intentionally put a system into place that secured higher wages for a special targeted group. However, when you peek beneath the compensation hood of many companies and industries, something systemic is going on.

OCCUPATIONAL SEGREGATION

Put simply, occupational segregation, one of the primary causes of wage gaps, is where there are male-dominated roles and where there are female-dominated roles. If you've ever stayed at a large hotel or resort, you've probably noticed that most of the people working on the grounds or doing maintenance on the property are men, and women do mostly the housekeeping duties. That's occupational segregation at its most basic level.

If you had met the general manager of that resort, you would have discovered a male in that role. That's occupational segregation at a deeper level.

Despite all the progress we've made, there is still a disproportionate number of women and people of color working in lower-paying positions and industries like childcare, education, and home healthcare. Meanwhile, the flip side of that is found in higher-paying roles in the finance and tech worlds, which men dominate.

PAY DISCRIMINATION

Even when women and people of color land in positions generally held by men, we find evidence of a second key factor contributing to wage gaps: pay discrimination. Again, I have never met anyone who said, "We like to pay the men at least $.17 more per dollar than the women." But, even though it's illegal, in the same way that spitting on the sidewalk is illegal, it still happens. Case in point in 2023, the EEOC filed charges against Lacey's Place, a gaming parlor company, for paying women less than their male counterparts and for firing a woman when she complained about it.

Thankfully, blatant discrimination is rare, and when it's discovered, it's dealt with, and the perpetrators are punished. Meanwhile, pay discrimination behind the scenes can be harder to find, and often that's because we're blind that we're doing it.

Many people develop unconscious biases concerning gender stereotypes when they are children. As adults, without realizing it, those biases may tilt them toward favoring male candidates for certain roles and women for others, which encourages occupational segregation. And, according to the Pew Research Center, these biases may also lead them to favor particular background data, which could explain why a pay gap persists for women and minorities (excluding Asian males) who have the same education and job history as white or Asian men.[1]

MOTHERHOOD AND CAREGIVING PENALTIES

There's an irony in this contributing factor, and that is, while women experience a "motherhood penalty" after giving birth, men often receive a "fatherhood bonus" when they become dads. Why? It's pure speculation, but most likely another (hopefully unconscious) bias causes employers to

---

1   Nikki Graf, Anna Brown, and Eileen Patten, "Gender Discrimination Comes in Many Forms for Today's Working Women," Pew Research Center, December 14, 2017, https://www.pewresearch.org/short-reads/2017/12/14/gender-discrimination-comes-in-many-forms-for-todays-working-women/.

view men as needing more financial resources to support their families. Meanwhile, employers believe women will be less available for longer days or more hours than men, should the need arise. They also think women will be less committed to their jobs after they have a baby. Perhaps compounding that perception is that women usually take on the responsibility for childcare and, as such, are often the parent who calls in sick because a child has a fever and cannot attend school.[2]

Parenting responsibilities aside, as women become part of the sandwich generation—when they have children at home and have a parent or two in need of extra support—the toll taken on their career trajectories can be enormous. Frequently, employers overlook them for promotions, and if they take a family medical leave for any reason, they risk a 79 percent chance of not receiving the same pay raises their peers do.[3]

NEGOTIATION AND STARTING SALARIES

I touched on this problem earlier in the book. Unfortunately, it's prevalent and consistent around the country. Women

---

2 Erin George, "Mothers' Employment Has Surpassed Pre-Pandemic Levels, but the Child Care Crisis Persists," U.S. Department of Labor Blog, May 6, 2024, https://blog.dol.gov/2024/05/06/mothers-employment-has-surpassed-pre-pandemic-levels-but-the-child-care-crisis-persists.

3 How Caregiving Responsibilities Impact Women in the Workplace," Homethrive, March 3, 2025, https://homethrive.com/blog/how-caregiving-responsibilities-impact-women-in-the-workplace/.

and people of color rarely negotiate their starting salaries. This is not a problem on the job seeker's part, however. Study after study has found that interviewers perceive women as difficult to work with when they negotiate for a higher salary.[4] During the interviewing process, women tend to believe they would negatively view negotiation. So, they choose not to.

Making things worse, women achieve less success when they negotiate, and some have even faced penalties for it.[5] Reports indicate they have experienced backlash. People are prejudiced against them as being difficult from the day they start their new position, which creates an uncomfortable working situation that's hard to overcome.

Regardless of why or what happened in the original salary negotiations, though, when anyone starts out being paid at a lower rate than others in their position, they can never catch up with typical annual raises and incentives. They are always behind the eight ball. And should they leave and go to another company, their salary history can follow them and be used to set their pay at the new job. This key factor contributing to wage disparities can perpetuate over time, and when you add in becoming a mother, the wage gap grows ever wider.

---

4   Hannah Riley Bowles, "Why Women Don't Negotiate Their Job Offers," *Harvard Business Review*, June 19, 2014, https://hbr.org/2014/06/why-women-dont-negotiate-their-job-offers.

5   "The Simple Truth About the Gender Pay Gap," AAUW, accessed March 2, 2026, https://www.aauw.org/resources/research/simple-truth/.

LACK OF TRANSPARENCY

Of course, if all companies behaved the way federal governing agencies do and were completely transparent regarding compensation, then most of the pay equity issues we have would disappear. Instead, many jobs are posted with no salary mentioned. Employees are encouraged to be discreet and not discuss their wages with each other. And only a handful of people within an organization are involved with salary decisions. Consequently, employees frequently do not know how they are paid in relation to others in similar positions. With such blinders in place, an employee could spend their entire working tenure with a company completely in the dark about how they are suffering a wage disparity.

If, however, those companies acted the way our government must for compensation, they would post each job with clear salary parameters, assign a non-violable pay rate range to every position, and provide complete transparency about who was being paid how much. Such measures and transparency prevent wage gaps from ever starting.

INTERSECTIONALITY

I touched on intersectionality when discussing occupational segregation previously. When we move beyond gender *or* race wage disparities to gender *and* race disparities, the wage gap grows at that intersection. At the time of this writing, according to the American Association of University Women's research, white women in the United States get paid eighty-three cents for each dollar a man earns.[6] That's bad enough, but Black women earn even less—just sixty-four cents per man-dollar. For Native American women, it's sixty cents, and for Latinas, it's only fifty-seven cents! That's right: Latina women make just a little over half of what white men do.

By this point, you can understand how many variables there are when figuring out why a wage gap exists. With no clear, definitive answer, you can see why it's hard for a company to initiate any one policy to address it. What they can do is just accept the fact that they have an equity problem and then find a solution to fix it. However, identifying the specific nature of the problem, and figuring out how big the gap is that must be closed, requires digging a little deeper into those rather alarming statistics I wrote about in the previous paragraph. Thankfully, we have plenty of resources to help us.

---

6   American Association of University Women, "The Simple Truth About the Gender Pay Gap: 2020 Update" (Washington, DC: AAUW, 2020).

MEASURING THE WAGE GAP: METHODOLOGIES AND DATA SOURCES

As with most statistics, there is more to the numbers than meets the eye when we talk about what women and minorities make compared to white males. Yes, when we put all non-Hispanic, white men working year-round full-time jobs in one bucket, and all women working year-round full-time jobs in another bucket, then average out their salaries, we see that for every dollar a man makes, a woman only makes eighty-three cents.

However, using such categories doesn't measure the actual wage gap. Because remember, occupational segregation is happening, so many of those women are filling lesser-paying roles than men. To get a better and more accurate idea of the disparity, dial in on the issue and look at it at the job level. There, you can get a clearer idea of what the wage gap is like for each position. That's what the state of California did when it enacted its Equal Pay Act.

That state's law requires companies to pay all employees the same amount of money based on their job functions. Regardless of sex, race, or ethnicity, if two people are doing "substantially similar work," then they must be paid equally. By zeroing in on the similar work aspect, California (and subsequent states' laws that followed their lead) looks at four different compensable factors, such as skill, effort, responsibility, and working conditions.

To see how that would look in the workplace, let's say there are forty women and five men working at a customer service representative level two for a company. Being "level two" requires specific skills, education, and experience, which they all have. They all also have to put in the same effort to get their work done because they have the same job responsibilities they perform under identical conditions. So, by law, because those compensable factors are similar, they should all be paid the same. But, if those five men average $55,000 a year and those forty women average $45,000, then there's a wage gap of $10,000 that the company will have to bridge. The gap in this example is actually a little worse than the numbers above, because in this scenario, the women make just eighty-one cents per dollar the men make.

There are some good and trustworthy sources of data that we can look at to help us see the true nature of the existing wage gaps. These include:

- **US Census Bureau:** Here you can find earnings data covering the entire United States broken out by gender, race, and other demographics.
- **Bureau of Labor Statistics (BLS):** As its name suggests, this organization focuses on wages and employment, providing statistical reports built from data about occupations, industries, and demographic characteristics.
- **Equal Employment Opportunity Commission**

(EEOC): Large, private companies—i.e., those employing more than one hundred employees—must file something called an EEO-one report with the EEOC every year. This organization then compiles and analyzes the reports to determine pay disparities based on gender, race, or ethnicity.

- **Private Sector Studies:** McKinsey, Payscale, Glassdoor, and other private groups keep tabs on what's happening in the working world through user-submitted salaries and other internal data they can source. They then provide detailed and insightful reports on a multitude of subjects, including wage gaps and disparities.
- **Academic Research:** Business schools and economic departments in universities across the country publish new peer-reviewed studies every year that provide context, analysis, and longitudinal insights on employee earnings and wage gaps.

While each of the above sources can help us get closer to the true nature of the wage gap, none are perfect or supply all the information we need. They can provide guidance for policymakers and employers, but we cannot know for sure what has been underreported or how limited the data sets are. Until all employers across the country can achieve pay equity within their respective organizations, the gap will remain, and we'll continue to have Equal Pay Day every spring.

EQUAL PAY DAY

The National Committee on Pay Equity (NCPE) created Equal Pay Day in 1996 to raise and maintain awareness about the wage gap in the United States. Falling on a different date each year, it represents how far into the new year women must work to earn what men earned in the previous year. The date changes because it is based on the size of the gap. Usually, it happens in March or April, and the larger the gap, the later it falls. At the time of this writing, women earned eighty-three cents for every dollar that men earned, and the holiday fell on March 25.

Many states recognize Equal Pay Day, and there are other forms of the day, too, which include Black Women's Equal Pay Day; Latina Equal Pay Day; Native Women's Equal Pay Day; and Asian American, Native Hawaiian, and Pacific Islander (AANHPI) Women's Equal Pay Day. You can probably guess that those days happen even later in the year than the general Equal Pay Day does, as they have even wider gaps to close.

Through rallies, panel discussions, social media campaigns (#EqualPayDay), and encouraging women to wear red (to symbolize being "in the red" financially), Equal Pay Day has gone beyond just raising awareness of the gap. It has actually been instrumental in getting the Paycheck Fairness Act approved and prompt policy changes to encourage pay transparency and wage audits.

LOOKING AHEAD

As important as Equal Pay Day is, we must remember that it is viewing the wage gap from the two-bucket perspective I mentioned previously: all women workers averaged out compared to all men.

To truly achieve pay equity, we must look at what the males, females, and different diversity groups are earning by comparing their wages at the job level, then paying the same amount to each person in similar jobs.

Will there still be a disparity between what all men in aggregate averaged out are making versus all women? Probably. But again, that comes back to what are the female-dominated roles versus the male-dominated roles, and how are those roles compensated? We cannot get equal pay to happen within that framework until we no longer have occupational segregation, or at least have levels of occupational segregation between the sexes be comparable. And yet, that still wouldn't touch on the impact of racial discrimination. Diverse groups and the indigenous are often living in poorer communities, which limits their education and possibility for advancement, and only perpetuates wage gaps. However, those issues, while extremely important, exceed the scope of this book.

My goal here is to show you how I get companies to achieve pay equity across all jobs. In the chapters that follow, we'll explore the legal frameworks governing pay equity, dive into organizational strategies for achieving fairness, and provide tools for measuring, communicating, and sustaining equitable pay practices.

The journey to equal pay starts with awareness—but it must lead to action.

CHAPTER 2

LEGISLATION FOR PAY EQUITY

While a few companies do reach out to my organization every year because they want to be sure they're paying their employees fairly, the vast majority of our clients come to us because they have to. They need our help because their state passed a new law, and now they are at risk of being fined if an employee should ever file a claim saying their employer did not disclose their salary range to them or, worse, if an employee discovered they were being paid less than others in their position without justification.

So far, twenty states have passed pay equity laws, and generally, I can tell when someone calls me if they are in one. Because as soon as the "Hello, how are you?" pleasantries are over, I'm hit with something like, "I'm behind the eight ball. I don't have any salary ranges. I have to defend what we are doing, and we don't even know what we're doing! How on Earth are we ever going to get compliant?" And there is panic in their voices.

That panic is understandable. Nobody wants to be on a list of noncompliance. It's bad for public relations, and having a state's attorney general breathing down your neck is never fun. To understand what companies must deal with, this chapter provides an overview of the key US federal laws that form the backbone of pay equity protections, examines innovative state and local initiatives, and explores how global policy trends are shaping the international conversation around equal pay.

KEY US FEDERAL LAWS: FLSA, EQUAL PAY ACT, TITLE VII, AND LILLY LEDBETTER

THE FAIR LABOR STANDARDS ACT (FLSA)

The Fair Labor Standards Act was passed in the middle of 1938. For the first time in our country's history, the United States had labor standards that, among other things, set minimum wage requirements and rules for paying overtime. We also had a new federal agency within the Department of Labor, the Wage and Hour Division, that was tasked with enforcing those standards.

What the FLSA did *not* do was include all categories of workers in its provisions. Unfortunately, domestic and agricultural laborers were excluded. So the people who could probably have benefited the most by having a guaranteed minimum wage, meaning the women and people of color who historically held those positions, were not protected. That early form of occupational segregation contributed greatly to the wage gap that persists today among those groups.

However, it was a solid first step toward equity because, now that we had some basic wage standards, the ground was set for wage disparity to become evident wherever it was lurking, which it inevitably did.

THE EQUAL PAY ACT OF 1963

When President John F. Kennedy signed the Equal Pay Act (EPA) into law in 1963, he made it illegal for companies to pay men and women differently for doing the same job—"same" meaning doing a job that is substantially equal in skill, effort, responsibility, and working conditions.[7] That was the first antidiscrimination law ever written to specifically protect women. Theoretically, employers would have to pay men and women the same, unless there was a difference in seniority, quantity or quality of products

---

7   Margaret Burke, "Lessons from Labor Feminists: Using Collective Action to Improve Conditions for Women Lawyers," *American University Journal of Gender, Social Policy & the Law* 26, no. 1 (2018): 559–592.

created, merit, or some other factor that had nothing to do with their gender.

However, getting theory to line up with reality proved harder than expected. Employers were able to use that "other factor" vagueness to include things like salary history or market demand at the time of hiring to justify a pay differential.

The EPA also fell short in two other important ways. The first concerns enforcement. That law left it up to the employee being discriminated against to provide proof that a wage disparity was evident. Because few (if any) companies had transparent pay policies, that burden of proof was often impossible to find. The second way it fell short was by not covering the disparities happening among people of color.

We needed something different. We needed something better. Enter Title VII.

TITLE VII OF THE CIVIL RIGHTS ACT OF 1964

In 1964, the folks in Washington realized there were still far too many people left unprotected in the country's workplaces. To that end, Title VII of the Civil Rights Act was passed to prohibit discrimination based on race, color, religion, gender, or national origin when it comes to compensation.[8] Notably absent from that bill was a requirement for jobs to be substantially similar.

The EEOC enforces Title VII. It also oversees the resolution of claims brought on by people who feel they've been discriminated against when it comes to pay or being promoted, or who feel their company is retaliating against them when they complained about unequal pay.

So within two years, we had the EPA and Title VII passed in an effort to eliminate wage discrimination. But they weren't enough, especially for folks like Lilly Ledbetter.

LILLY LEDBETTER FAIR PAY ACT OF 2009

What some people consider to be one of the biggest failures of Title VII is that it limited the window for employees to sue for pay discrimination to 180 days after they received their first paycheck. Somehow, within the first six months of being employed in a company, a worker is supposed to be able to discover and prove that wage discrimination is going on.

Lilly Ledbetter certainly didn't know it was happening at her company when she accepted a job there. She

---

8   Shane Phillips, "A Text-based Interpretation of Title VII's Religious-Employer Exemption," *Texas Review of Law & Politics* 20, no. 2 (2016): 295–340.

learned nineteen years later. As she approached retirement, she received an anonymous note saying she was being paid—and had been paid during her entire tenure of her career—thousands less than her male peers were. In fact, over the course of her career, she'd received about $200,000 less![9] She sued. Her case went all the way to the Supreme Court...and she lost, due to the 180-day clause. However, her situation gained so much attention that the Lilly Ledbetter Act of 2009 was enacted, which opened that statute of limitation window for pay discrimination much wider.

At this point in our legislative history, you'd think that we have the laws we need to ensure fair wages are paid to everyone. Yet that's still not happening. For whatever reason, many companies are ignoring the federal laws. Thankfully, several states have noticed and have started picking up the slack.

STATE AND LOCAL PAY EQUITY AND SALARY TRANSPARENCY LAWS

The various state laws seem to have more teeth to them than the federal ones—the states include fines and penalties for any violations, and the attorneys general are not

---

9   Trip Gabriel and Claire Moses, "Lilly Ledbetter, Who Fought for Equal Pay, Dies at 86," *New York Times*, October 14, 2024, https://www.nytimes.com/2024/10/14/obituaries/lilly-ledbetter-dead.html.

bashful when it's time to collect. California led the way by being the first state to create a pay equity law when it mandated employers with more than fifteen employees to include pay ranges in job ads and to provide that information to any current employee who asks to see it. Colorado soon followed up with a law that demands salary ranges to be included on *all* position postings, even remote positions.

Next thing you know, New York jumped on the bandwagon by requiring salary ranges for jobs that are either performed in that state or for positions that report to a supervisor located there. And then other states chimed in, including my state, Massachusetts. Here, employers with more than twenty-five employees must include the salary range in all job postings and, like California, they must provide those ranges to any current employee who asks to see them.

Now, twenty states have enacted good, strong pay equity laws with stiff penalties for violations, and fourteen states have salary transparency requirements. What's making these laws so effective is the fact that the attorneys general in those states are making examples out of companies that are not compliant. Fines and penalties are fierce! While that's bad enough, what could possibly be an even worse consequence of noncompliance is the fallout on social media as experienced by some larger corporations in New York City. They had posted extremely broad salary ranges for open positions, then were lambasted online as people called them out on it for trying to circumvent the law. Subsequently, their salary ranges drastically narrowed.

While each state (and some cities) has unique aspects to their laws, many share similar elements like salary history bans and pay transparency requirements, and others are creating pay equity laws.

Salary history bans. Right now, almost half the states in the US prohibit employers from asking job candidates about their salary history. They also ban the use of previous compensation to justify how much a company will pay the candidate in their new posotion, should they make them an offer. This ban is probably one of the most effective ways to put an end to pay inequity, one person at a time.

Pay Transparency Requirements. If you've been looking at job postings recently, you may have noticed that more and more of them are including the salary range for open positions. That is because numerous states have enacted laws requiring them to do so. Gone are the days of candidates applying blind to their potential income, and even better, everyone applying knows the floor and ceiling salary for that position, as does the rest of the company's employees, which greatly inhibits pay disparity from salary negotiations at the outset.

State Pay Equity Acts. In an acknowledgment that the federal Equal Pay Act wasn't going far enough, many states have passed enhanced pay equity acts that exceed the fed's mandates in ways that favor the employees more. For example, most of them insist the work must be "comparable" rather than "equal." What that means is the work must be substantially similar in skill, effort, and responsibility. Also, it must be performed under similar working conditions.

Going even further, many states put the burden of proof squarely on the employers and not the employees, and they punish employers who retaliate against employees for discussing wages among themselves.

While the above seems to suggest that it's always the companies that are the bad actors, there are some provisions for organizations that are trying to do the right thing. For example, in Massachusetts, employers who proactively dig in, do an equity analysis, and make progress toward fixing their issues are protected from being sued by employees for pay disparities.

So we can easily see that, despite the idea for pay equity originating at the federal level of the government, the new standards set at the state level are sweeping the country with change. As more and more states come on board with the concept, perhaps the nation as a whole will finally achieve pay equity reform.

For employers who hire remote workers, there is something

else to keep in mind here. That is, you must abide by the laws that govern the states where your employees live, So, if your headquarters are in Florida, where there is no specific law separate from federal mandates, and you have a remote workforce with employees in Rhode Island and California, you must abide by the laws in Rhode Island for your employees there and in California for your employees there. Similarly, regardless of where your company is located in the United States, if you employ remote workers who live in other countries, you must abide by those countries' laws.

Let's take a look at what's happening around the globe, now, to give you an idea of what you can expect.

INTERNATIONAL COMPARISONS AND GLOBAL POLICY TRENDS

I guess it's true that misery loves company, because the US is not, by far, the only country with pay equity issues. It's a global phenomenon. However, we are also not alone in trying to fix the problem. In fact, many countries are proving to be a little more innovative than we are and have put into place mandates and laws that go beyond what we're doing here in the States. The strongest statutes are currently found in Europe and Canada.

UNITED KINGDOM: PAY GAP REPORTING

Beginning in 2017, companies in the United Kingdom that employ more than 250 people are required to complete an Annual Survey of Hours and Earnings (ASHE), which publicly discloses all the dirty details found in their gender pay gap statistics. The ASHE reports include all bonus disparities and the mean and median wage gaps. Something else that's interesting, and that so far is unique to that country, is that the companies must also report the proportions of men versus women in each pay quartile.

These annual reports create transparency regarding pay scales within those countries as well as encourage accountability—the public is not shy about discussing what they find in those reports! Statistics to date suggest this strategy is a successful one. From 2017 to 2024, the pay gap has declined from 18.4 percent—meaning women were paid, on average, 18.4 percent less than men—to 13.1 percent among full-time workers.[10]

ICELAND: MANDATORY PAY AUDITS

Following on the heels of the UK, in 2018, Iceland became the first country to insist on mandatory pay equity audits and certifications. Under their new rules, any company

---

10   Office for National Statistics, "Gender Pay Gap in the UK: 2024," October 29, 2024, https://www.ons.gov.uk/employmentandlabourmarket/peopleinwork/earningsandworkinghours/bulletins/genderpaygapintheuk/2024.

employing on average more than twenty-five people must have an independent audit conducted on their wages every three years. If they pass the audit, they will receive an Equal Pay Certificate. If they do not pass and are found noncompliant, then the company will be fined.

The initiative is considered successful. Before it began, Iceland had an unadjusted wage gap of 13.6 percent, and it has shrunk that gap by 9.3 percent in 2023.[11]

CANADA: PAY EQUITY ACTS

Perhaps because of its geographical size, similar to the United States, Canada enforces pay equity at both the federal and provincial levels. That country enacted its Federal Pay Equity Act in 2021, which applies to companies in federally regulated industries with more than ten employees. Federally regulated industries in Canada include finance, transportation, infrastructure, postal, communications, government offices, and parliamentary institutions.

The act's directives also require employers to periodically evaluate to determine whether pay inequity is happening in jobs held predominantly by women. Yes, they are trying to address occupational segregation! The companies must

---

11 Statistics Iceland, "Unadjusted Gender Pay Gap 2023," September 11, 2024, https://statice.is/publications/news-archive/social-affairs/unadjusted-gender-paygap-2023/.

compare the female-dominated jobs, such as customer service, with male-dominated ones, like maintenance, to ensure both groups are paid equitably.

Currently, the jury is still out on whether this act has made a difference. It's considered too soon to know for sure, right now. However, most believe it's a positive "step in the right direction."[12]

EUROPEAN UNION: PAY TRANSPARENCY DIRECTIVE

A trickle-down effect of the European Union creating the Euro area can be seen in wage and labor rules being codified and enforced throughout the region. It makes sense if you think about it. If everyone is being paid in the same currency, and if that currency is going to have a stable value throughout the territory, then there should be unity and consistency in how people in that area are being paid.

To that end, the EU approved a directive in 2023 that requires companies in all member states to post the starting salaries in all job ads and provide employees with the right to request wage data for their own and similar positions.

---

12   Moira Potter, "Has the Federal Pay Equity Act Helped to Close Canada's Gender Pay Gap?," *Benefits Canada*, September 15, 2023, https:// www.benefitscanada.com/archives_/benefits-canada-archive/ has-the-federal-pay-equity-act-helped-to-close-canadas-gender-pay-gap/.

Perhaps most applicable to what we're talking about in this book, those companies must also do an analysis to uncover potential pay gaps, report any that are found, and if they exceed 5 percent, then those companies must take action to rectify the situation.

The EU's directive left it up to the various member states to write their own laws for how they will implement these changes within their countries and is allowing for the phasing in of these changes. Most member states expect to be in complete compliance by mid-2026. So we probably won't see massive change or reform until later in the 2020s.

TOWARD STRONGER PROTECTIONS

As you can see, pay equity isn't just an idea we're putting into action in the US. Many countries have recognized both the need and the potential benefits of such innovative practices as transparency, accountability, and proactive audits. Despite the fears of going through the process to uncover and then rectify pay equity, companies do come out on the other side in a much better place—reduced lawsuits, better employee morale, lower turnover rates, and even better production all result when pay equity is achieved.

So, are you ready to get started? Let's begin by looking at how to create internal equity.

CHAPTER 3

HOW TO CREATE INTERNAL EQUITY

At this point in the book, you may have noticed a slight shift in the language as I discussed the evolution of wage laws. At the beginning, the use of the term "equal" is frequently found, but as I progressed, "equity" began popping up more often. In this chapter, we'll make another shift to look at internal equity. The terms may be similar, but there are inherent differences among them. So, before I continue to explore internal equity, it might be a good idea to clarify what all these words really mean.

EQUAL PAY

When using the phrase "equal pay," we're talking about paying employees who are doing substantially similar work for the same amount of money, regardless of their gender, race, or other demographic characteristics.

Equal pay is relatively easy to achieve. You assign a value to a job, then pay every single person who performs that job the same amount of money to start, and then apply the same formula for pay increases over time.

PAY EQUITY

Pay equity expands on the concept of equal pay to focus on achieving fairness by removing the potential for pay disparities, even when the work is not the same or substantially similar. Equity also takes into consideration a job's value, the market rate for the position, and demographic disparities.

To achieve pay equity, we must audit organizations to determine if there are unexplained pay gaps between or among genders or races across different jobs. If any are found, we analyze why they are there, address any biases that may influence pay decisions, and ensure everyone is fairly compensated based on their contributions and the value of their jobs.

For example, let's say an audit reveals you're paying a male financial analyst $10,000 a year more than a female with the same title. At first glance, that might look like a pay disparity based on gender, right? But we cannot know for sure until we take a deeper dive into compensable factors for both in their positions. Do they have similar experience levels? Have comparable skills? Need to put in the same amount of effort? Hold parallel responsibilities?

If the compensable factors for both positions *are* similar, then we can say "Yes! There's pay discrimination going on here, and we need pay equity." However, if, for some reason, the female financial analyst has a lighter responsibility load, so she doesn't need the same level of skills or experience (nor does she have them), then paying her less could still align with achieving pay equity. (Though you may want to be aware of the potential for occupational segregation here.)

INTERNAL EQUITY

When we use the phrase "internal equity," we move the discussion from the general concept of pay equity to its specific application within an organization. Internal equity is all about fairness in pay among employees within the same organization, based on their jobs' relative value.

For example, if your HR manager and your accounting manager are at the same level of your company's organizational chart, and they contribute similarly to the business, then there should *not* be a significant difference in their pay.

Internal equity is the focus of this chapter, as it is the crux of all pay equity initiatives. It is the foundation you will use to create a fair pay structure.

WHY DOES INTERNAL EQUITY MATTER?

Suppose you are in one of the forty states that have laws on the books mandating pay equity. In that case, you already have one reason why internal equity matters: Unless you achieve it, your organization will be at risk for fines and penalties. But even if you are not worried about any such legal measures, achieving internal equity will benefit your company in immeasurable ways.

TRUST AND MORALE

For starters, internal equity helps build and maintain the trust your employees have in your company as well as the stability of their morale. Among the last things any organization would want to deal with is the aftermath of employees discovering they are being paid less for doing similar work than their colleagues. And there's nothing a company can do to prevent them from finding out.

The National Labor Relations Act established standards that prohibit companies from forbidding employees from discussing their wages, their coworkers' wages, or even the wages of their supervisors or managers. And some states, like New Jersey, go even further by having laws that prohibit companies from retaliating or disciplining employees for doing so.

While you don't *have* to encourage your employees to discuss their wages, there's nothing you can do to prevent them from having those conversations. And should they start talking about their pay, and you haven't completed an audit to find and address any potential pay disparity issues, well, things could get ugly.

Thanks to the Lilly Ledbetter Act, you could be sued. But even if it doesn't go that far, you will lose the trust of your employees. You'll risk them perceiving you as a company that doesn't have their best interests at heart, which in turn will breed resentment. If they can't trust you to be honest with them about their pay, they'll wonder if they can trust you with anything. Disengagement will set in, and "quiet quitting" or even blatant resignations can ramp up. Then, in the world of social media, as they walk out the door, it's very possible they'll spread the word as to why they're leaving to anyone thinking of replacing them.

LEGAL COMPLIANCE

Even if your employees don't discuss their wages, a lack of internal equity can still be discovered. Internal factors, like employee complaints about incorrect pay or unpaid overtime, and internal audits for various government compliance initiatives, can trigger pay audits. And externally, things like audits from the Department of Labor or the IRS might turn up evidence of inequity.

When inequity is exposed via these means, there is little a company can do to protect itself from the legal ramifications. Penalties from the Equal Pay Act can come in the form of fines from the EEOC for up to $10,000, imprisonment for up to six months, or both. In cases where it's deemed the employer "willfully" violated the act, they may be forced to reward employees who'd been unfairly paid with double the amount of back pay.[13]

And let's not forget the power of the states. While each state has its own fee and punishment structure, no state attorney general takes kindly to wage equity violations.

ORGANIZATIONAL CULTURE

It's generally accepted that an employee's behavior and productivity are correlated with the corporate culture. The more positive and healthy a work culture is, the happier and more positive the employees, which translates to improved

---

13   U.S. Equal Employment Opportunity Commission, "Remedies for Employment Discrimination," accessed March 2, 2026, https://www.eeoc.gov/remedies-employment-discrimination.

performance, better productivity, and fewer days absent from work.[14]

A key component for creating a good work culture is internal equity. By ensuring everyone is paid fairly and justly, you are proving to your employees that you value them and their contributions. Extending beyond the current workforce, in today's world, where everything is shared on social media and in the ever-increasing "best of" or "most happy" lists, it's hard, if not impossible, for a company without internal equity to get a foothold on being respected. Meanwhile, by improving their corporate culture through internal equity, organizations become more attractive to better candidates, potential investors, clients, or other business relationships.

JOB EVALUATION METHODS TO ASSESS RELATIVE JOB VALUE

Now that you're convinced it's time to create internal equity, your first question is probably "Where do I start?" My answer to that is, "With job evaluations." If the goal of internal equity is to pay people a fair and just wage for their job, then the first thing you need to do is determine the value of their jobs.

---

14   "Why Workplace Culture Matters," Harvard Division of Continuing Education Professional & Executive Development, accessed March 2, 2026, https://professional.dce.harvard.edu/blog/why-workplace-culture-matters/.

Doing job evaluations first might be a bit surprising. After all, we're discussing paying people, so it's within reason that you could be expected to evaluate the person doing the job. However, equity is about paying people the same for doing jobs that are similar in scope and that require a similar background or experience. So evaluating the job, assessing its relative value to the organization, is where you start determining how much to pay every person who does that job.

Job evaluations must be done through a structured, logical, and objective process. Additionally, you'll want to be consistent in the way you do the evaluations across all the positions within your organization. Consistency is key here—ultimately, you'll want to use a framework that you can apply to each position to make the process simpler for yourself. Why reinvent the wheel with each job you focus on when you could use a replicable process that would still be viable when it's time to reevaluate or add new jobs in the future?

Luckily for us all, there are already a few tried-and-true methods available to use, so we don't have to create something new. We'll look at them now and discuss the pros and cons of each.

1. RANKING METHOD

One of the less complex and simpler job evaluation methods is the ranking method. Here, organizations will frequently have a committee of people who review each job to determine its overall importance to the company and then rank those positions from highest to lowest.

The core four compensable factors form the basis of the evaluations. Each job will be looked at through the lens of those factors and sorted so that similar jobs are put into the same buckets.

Once that is done, the buckets will be given a label that references them, whether that's job titles, an assigned letter or number, or something more basic like "unskilled," "semi-skilled," or "skilled."

When all jobs are sorted and labeled, the process of ranking from most important to least important can begin.

Pros:

- Because it is so simple, the ranking method can be one of the quickest to implement.
- It works beautifully for small businesses with few employees who have distinct responsibilities.
- It is inexpensive to do.
- Employees easily understand how their jobs are evalu-

ated and can see where they fit within the organization's hierarchy.

Cons:

- Even though the same core factors are being used to evaluate the jobs, there is plenty of room for subjective judgment and bias to come into play.
- There is no clear rationale for the rankings, which could create friction and confusion among employees who have different opinions regarding the worth of their jobs. Even if the people in the decision-making seats can be fair in their judgment, it can be difficult to explain why one job is more valuable than another.
- Large organizations with multiple different jobs and different levels within each job would find the process unwieldy and next to impossible to accurately rank all positions.

2. CLASSIFICATION METHOD

For readers with experience in government or unionized organizations, the classification method will be familiar, as it is often applied in those settings. This method first requires that categories or grades of jobs be defined based on the compensable factors. Then, each job is analyzed by comparing its compensable factors with those found within the different categories. Once the closest match is discovered, the job is assigned to that category or grade, which then determines the pay range.

Pros:

- Another simple method. Because it provides clear levels, it should be easy to see where jobs rank once they are assigned to a category.
- Once it is set up, it can be easy to administer, so any new jobs created after the system is in place can simply be slotted into an appropriate category.
- Because it is so systematized, it is easier to develop a consistent pay structure to use from that point on.

Cons:

- The system is often seen as too rigid or inflexible. As jobs evolve or new, unique ones are created, sometimes they do not fit nicely within the predefined categories.
- This is a much more time-consuming method than the ranking method! There is quite a bit of preplanning and decision-making that needs to happen before you can even start to use the process. Additionally, as the organization changes and evolves, the method will need to be evaluated and possibly adjusted.
- It leaves you open to the potential for dissimilar jobs being placed in the same categories or grades.

3. POINT FACTOR METHOD

The point factor method is possibly the most objective and consistent method we have for job evaluation. It provides a very structured way of quantifying the value of a job by assigning points to each of the compensable factors.

First, each compensable factor (again, the skill, effort, responsibility, and working conditions required for someone to be successful in their position) is broken down into levels that reflect the potential scope of the factor, and then each level is assigned a number of points reflecting the intensity of that level. For example, skill could be broken down into beginner, which could be assigned ten points; intermediate, assigned twenty; and expert, assigned thirty. Responsibility levels could be low, medium, or high. Effort would be related to the intensity required for the job. Working conditions would be ranked from safest to most hazardous or unpleasant.

Because few jobs are created where the compensable factors are equally important, the factors should also be weighted to reflect their importance in relation to the overall job worth. For example, an intermediate-level graphic designer would have skills weighted the most, maybe at forty percent, responsibility and effort would be about equal at twenty-five percent each, then working conditions at ten percent.

Once all jobs have their points assigned for each level, those values are then multiplied by the weight to get a weighted point value for each factor. All of those are then added up for the total points of the job.

You're not quite done! Next, use the total points to create a job hierarchy, grouping jobs with similar points as you do so. Once you form those groups, which are often called job grades, you will assign a pay level to each one.

Pros:

- Again, this is probably the most objective of the job evaluation methods.
- It makes being transparent easy.
- Because of its consistency, it is easy to determine where new jobs or jobs whose core factors have changed would align in the pay grades.

Cons:

- Time! While it's one of the most objective methods, it is also one of the most time-consuming to implement.
- Because each compensable factor is broken down into various levels, thorough definitions need to be created to justify the points, which means quite a bit of documentation will be involved and necessary to maintain.
- This method often requires specific training by consultants.

ALIGNING COMPENSATION WITH INTERNAL JOB WORTH

At this point, you now know how to analyze jobs to determine a rank for each one in terms of salary. You know which positions in your organization get paid more than others, and you have a rationale for why that is.

Now it's time to do that thing that might seem painful to do: figure out exactly how much money to pay the people in those job rankings. This is where the rubber meets the road, and internal equity is quantified through dollars.

I cannot get into specifics down to the penny here—or even to the dollar. That's because developing a pay structure requires not only understanding the relative importance of each job within your organization, but also your company's identified compensation philosophy—your pay strategy that includes base wages, benefits, and how those align with your values and goals. Both will be vastly different for each organization. However, there are generalized steps to figure out how to do this in an equitable manner.

STEP 1: DEVELOP JOB GRADES OR PAY BANDS

Depending on which job evaluation method you use, you will already be in the middle of this step. To finish it, look at the way you have your job positions grouped by point values or classification. For each one, break them down a little further into grades (some organizations like to use the word "bands") that you will use to define the salary ranges. The most typical grades include:

- **Minimum:** The lowest salary that will be paid for the job
- **Midpoint:** Market rate for employees who are fully competent in their job performance
- **Maximum:** The rate for your highly experienced or top-performing employees

Once you've done this for all jobs across your organization, you'll have a structure in place that will be both consistent and flexible. Hence, as employees improve in competency, you will be able to appropriately move them up the pay scale.

STEP 2: CONDUCT PAY EQUITY AND COMPRESSION ANALYSES

I take back what I said earlier...*now*, is where the rubber meets the road. Once you have the job pay grades figured out, it's time to look at what exactly you're currently paying your employees in each of those roles. Here, you'll do an audit where you'll analyze where each of your current employees falls within their respective ranges, collecting data on how much they are paid and what pay grade they are in.

Look for:

- **Inequities:** Are individuals in similar roles being paid differently without valid justification?
- **Compression:** Are new hires earning the same as or more than experienced employees?
- **Gaps by demographic:** Are there patterns that indicate gender or racial disparities?

As you can see, this is not a matter of creating a simple spreadsheet. You'll need to track wages, length of employment, the employees' levels of each compensable factor, and demographic information. Only by getting that complete picture will you be able to use a statistical tool to do an evaluation by job, department, and demographics to identify any disparities.

STEP 3: CREATE POLICIES FOR CONSISTENT PAY DECISIONS

Should any disparities be found, you'll want to investigate to find out how and why they happened. Doing so will help you create and establish a strategy to prevent them from continuing into the future. That strategy will be part of your overall compensation system, and should include:

- **Guidelines for starting pay:** Remember, a person's salary history should have nothing to do with what they are paid in your company. Offers to new hires should be based on the candidate's qualifications and where they fit in your job pay grades.

- **Promotion and adjustment criteria:** When you create the pay grades, in essence, you are defining the parameters around how employees will be eligible for promotion and increases.
- **Review cycles:** The only way you can be sure that your pay grades are evolving in ways that are consistent with the organization's growth and evolution is to regularly conduct reviews to ensure pay grades and wages remain aligned with internal and external factors.

Ultimately, your goal is to create a consistent but not rigid pay structure. Every company will want to maintain some wage flexibility to be able to shift when the market shifts or to reward the exceptional performance of a team member. Consistency doesn't preclude that flexibility, but it does ensure internal equity is maintained throughout the life of the organization.

INTERNAL EQUITY AS A STRATEGIC ADVANTAGE

Hopefully, by now, you can see how creating internal equity isn't something that should be done only to stay in compliance with state and federal laws. Instead, I hope you see it as a strategic business imperative, one that will improve employee morale and productivity and help your company maintain its competitive edge.

To recap what I mentioned earlier, internal equity supports:

- **Stronger retention:** Fair pay builds loyalty and reduces costly turnover.
- **Talent attraction:** Candidates are more likely to join organizations that demonstrate pay transparency and equity.
- **Cultural alignment:** Pay practices reflect and reinforce an organization's values.

And yes, it does protect you against the potential for expensive and time-consuming litigation. By achieving internal equity, your organization is taking a proactive step, rather than being forced into a reactive defense. Instead of discovering after the fact from official complaints or audits that you have pay disparities, you can design a system that discovers it yourself and fixes the situation, or nips it in the bud and begins promoting fairness from the start.

Of course, that system should also help your company stay competitive in your industry. So let's look next at how to develop a compensation system that will help you do that.

DEVELOPING A MARKET COMPETITIVE COMPENSATION SYSTEM

Now that you have internal equity figured out, let's expand beyond the organization to talk about external equity.

External equity looks at how a company's pay rates for different jobs compare to those of other employers with similar positions in their market. By achieving external equity, organizations remain competitive as they recruit new employees or create pathways of advancement for current ones.

WHY MARKET COMPETITIVENESS MATTERS

Many of the larger Silicon Valley companies have developed creative strategies to make working for them attractive—nap pods, free ice cream and snacks, on-site gyms, and even game rooms. The idea behind those innovations is to create environments where their employees can take mental breaks when needed and otherwise feel valued and wanted. While those strategies sound like great ideas, and maybe they are, the number one reason people will leave a job has nothing to do with whether they can take a nap after a carb-laden lunch. It's because they feel their pay is too low.[15]

Salary is also a primary concern for people looking for a new job. Sure, they might love the idea of a flexible schedule or on-site childcare, but if the pay isn't enough, they will pass on a position for one that pays better.[16] So, achieving internal equity isn't enough. Yes, that will help your current and future employees feel confident they are being paid fairly within your organization, but they also need to know that your fair pay aligns with what others in your industry or region are paying for their position. And that is what external equity can do for you.

---

15   Kim Parker and Juliana Menasce Horowitz, "Majority of Workers Who Quit a Job in 2021 Cite Low Pay, No Opportunities for Advancement, Feeling Disrespected," Pew Research Center, March 9, 2022, https://www.pewresearch.org/short-reads/2022/03/09/majority-of-workers-who-quit-a-job-in-2021-cite-low-pay-no-opportunities-for-advancement-feeling-disrespected/.

16   Ipsos, "Salary and Location Most Important to Americans When Deciding on a Job," news release, June 24, 2022, https://www.ipsos.com/en-us/news-polls/salary-and-location-most-important-americans-when-deciding-job.

You can achieve external equity by creating a market-competitive compensation system. Without one, you'll never be able to know for sure if your pay levels do align with the prevailing rates for similar jobs at companies within your region or industry. So let's look at how to do that now, which begins with finding the right data and understanding what it is telling us.

GATHERING AND ANALYZING MARKET COMPENSATION DATA

Finding wage data might seem like an easy thing to do. Why not just ask your employees or do an informal survey of your colleagues? I'll tell you why *NOT*: It's illegal. The DOL considers that kind of practice to be a form of price fixing or collusion. Regardless of your good intentions behind asking the questions and using the answers to form a compensation structure, the DOL will believe you're trying to artificially keep the wages low in your industry.

Case in point: Back in 2015, some tech giants had to pay $415 million to settle a lawsuit after being charged with price-fixing employee salaries and agreeing not to "poach" employees from each other.[17]

---

17   Aarti Shahani, "Tech Giants Will Pay $415 Million to Settle Employees' Lawsuit," NPR, January 16, 2015, https://www.npr.org/sections/alltechconsidered/2015/01/16/377614477/tech-giants-will-pay-415-million-to-settle-employees-lawsuit.

So, I encourage you to play it safe by using data from an outside source.

SOURCES OF MARKET DATA

You have a number of options for compensation data source material. Each will have unique strengths and limitations. Those sources include third-party salary surveys, crowd-sourced data, industry- or trade-specific surveys, or other custom compensation surveys. Regardless of which you wind up using, always remember that you're not just looking at numbers to determine salary ranges. You'll want to consider total compensation, including benefits and any bonuses.

THIRD-PARTY SURVEYS

You're probably familiar with these kinds of surveys, as they're often conducted by large, well-known consulting firms, associations, or vendors. Their data is often used in online articles or white papers related to HR or compensation. Mercer's annual Compensation Best Practices Report is probably one of the more famous of these surveys. Other frequently referenced ones include those completed by Willis Towers Watson, Radford, and Culpepper.

These surveys usually cover a broad spectrum of compensation subjects. Of course, they talk about salaries, including base pay, salary budgets, and structure, and they'll include information on variable pay like incentive plans, bonuses, commissions, and overtime compensation. They'll also go into benefits, performance management, and even look at tangential subjects like work–life balance, flexible work options, and company car policies. It will be important to stay focused on what, exactly, you're looking for. It's easy to go down interesting rabbit holes, maybe having nothing to do with the task at hand: Achieving external equity.

Generally, these reports are accessed by purchasing subscriptions, which can get pricey. However, they are considered the gold standard in compensation data.

CROWDSOURCED COMPENSATION DATA

As online platforms like Glassdoor, Payscale, and LinkedIn jockey to position themselves as the go-to resource for business professionals, they've become more and more involved in gathering employment and compensation data. The reports they put together are built out of self-reported data that individuals volunteer to share about their salaries, benefits, and other compensation topics. That data is then aggregated to create real-time analysis that is updated regularly as new submissions are collected.

There are a number of benefits to using these types of surveys. They are often useful for gaining directional insights, as the data is always fresh and trends can be identified more easily while they are happening. They cover a wide variety of industries, so whatever niche you're in will most likely be covered. Also, they're usually free, and who doesn't like free?

However, as with everything that may seem too good to be true, there are downsides. The biggest one is probably that the accuracy of the data is not always guaranteed—it is self-reported, after all. There is no data validation, and the data may not include specific job roles or account for company context when defining them.

INDUSTRY OR TRADE ASSOCIATION SURVEYS

These kinds of surveys are typically favored when you want to get compensation data that's targeted to specific sectors—for example, healthcare, nonprofits, and tech—providing data that might not apply to other, more generalized organizations. Such competitive benchmarking is a great benefit for building strategies to attract and retain talent.

Another way that industry or trade association surveys are helpful is that they can be used to help companies ensure they are creating compensation practices that are consistent with industry standards and legal compliance. A few of the more well-known sources are the Medical Professional Liability Association (MPL), the American Society of Association Executives, and the ASA Staffing.

Downsides to these surveys are that they don't apply to everyone. Their inherent nature means they are for targeted groups or industries. They are also subscription-based and must be purchased every year.

CUSTOM COMPENSATION SURVEYS

When you want something even more targeted than an industry or trade survey, so that you can get insight into niche roles or unique market segments, then you'll want access to a custom compensation survey. These tailored surveys are often designed for a company or consortium of companies to gather detailed compensation data on the salaries, benefits, and variable pay that is specific to them.

If you have niche roles or unique market segments, one of these surveys could be just what you need. Because they are so targeted, you don't have to rely on information from more generalized surveys that you then must figure out how to skew for your situation. They're also good for when you need to address a specific issue—like when a pay equity problem was discovered in a particular job role.

You can often get a custom compensation survey through one of the major compensation providers like WTW, Mercer, or Radford.

BEST PRACTICES FOR USING MARKET DATA

Whatever you use for your data, there are a few best practices to keep in mind as you analyze the survey and apply it to your organization.

- **Match jobs carefully:** Context is key here—what you include in a job description or how you define it might differ greatly from other companies. Go back to the compensable factors as you do your data analysis, and be sure that you're matching the job content, not just the titles. That will be the only way you'll be sure you are using comparable positions.

- **Use multiple sources:** I realize some of the market data sources can be expensive, but by relying on just one, you risk skewed results. Try your best to cross-reference positions across more than one source whenever possible. Remember, some of this data you can get for free from crowdsourced surveys.

- **Adjust for geography:** It makes sense that executive assistants working in major metropolitan cities get paid more than those working in small towns far from interstate highways. The cost of labor in your regional market needs to be a factor you consider when looking at salary ranges.

- **Adjust for organizational size:** Similar to above, executive assistants working for CEOs of large conglomerates often get paid more than those who work for small companies. The scale and complexity of your organization impact the responsibilities and expectations of your employees, and as such, should be taken into consideration when determining salaries.

- **Update regularly:** I don't have to tell you this; you already know: The labor market changes fast! Don't get complacent or think this exercise is a one-and-done. Expect to review your compensation data annually.

BENCHMARKING POSITIONS AND MAINTAINING COMPETITIVENESS

Once your market data is collected, the next step is benchmarking, which is where you'll actually go through the process of comparing your internal roles with the market data. This is the point where you discover whether you are competitive within your market, and if not, how much you'll need to adjust your salary ranges.

STEP 1: IDENTIFY BENCHMARK JOBS

First, you'll need to figure out which are your benchmark jobs. These are the positions that are commonly found across organizations. They're usually so well-defined or have such similar responsibilities that when someone says this is what they do at work, everyone knows exactly what they mean. They are jobs like:

- Accountant
- Customer service representative
- Software engineer
- HR generalist

These types of jobs are almost always included in market surveys, so you should be able to benchmark 60 to 70 percent of your roles using the data from those surveys to create your salary ranges.

Unique, niche, or hybrid positions can be tricky. If you have positions that are not easily aligned with your survey results, you'll need to get a little creative. Perhaps there will be two or more positions you can combine to create a proxy that will match your role.

STEP 2: ANALYZE MARKET POSITIONING

What you do for this step depends on your company's pay or compensation philosophy. I touched on pay philosophy in the last chapter. To expand on that here, you could also say that your pay philosophy puts your company into one of three buckets that reflect your strategic decisions about how you want to pay relative to the market:

- Pay below the market rate
- Pay at the market rate
- Pay above the market rate

Not all companies are in such a fiscal position where they can pay at or above market rates. For those organizations, I suggest they try to pay at least 10 percent below market but make up the difference by offering great benefits. Most employees or potential candidates won't be upset by a 10 percent difference if they're offered top-tier benefits such as good health insurance, life insurance, a 401(k), etc.

Also, your company philosophy doesn't have to be an all-or-nothing approach. Depending on the level of the job's importance or the difficulty of filling it, you may want to vary the pay rate accordingly. Perhaps you'll lead the market for your highly specialized technical positions but match it for your administrative support.

STEP 3: CREATE AND CALIBRATE SALARY RANGES

At this point, you have your job grades or levels defined, your benchmarked jobs, and your compensation philosophy figured out. So now it's time to create salary ranges for the job grades. Typically, organizations will create three different ranges:

- Minimum, paying 80 to 85 percent of the market rate
- Midpoint, paying at the market
- Maximum, paying 115 to 120 percent above the market

By using such ranges, your organization will have the flexibility to reward performance, give raises to award tenure, or adjust positively for new hires with stronger experience than required for the position.

STEP 4: MONITOR AND MAINTAIN

I realize this process can sound complex, difficult, and time-consuming. And honestly, sometimes it is. That's why it's important to document how you complete it, so that you can create a system to make it easier and smoother when it's time to repeat it. Because you will need to repeat it. The whole point of it is to allow your organization to stay competitive in the market. No industry is static. You'll want to stay on top of the data and be willing to adjust your salary ranges whenever conditions merit it. Those conditions include:

- Market movements
- Internal promotions and job changes
- Shifts in supply and demand for specific roles
- Inflation and economic conditions

By conducting regular compensation audits, you'll always be as competitive in your market as possible.

BALANCING INTERNAL EQUITY WITH EXTERNAL MARKET COMPETITIVENESS

In the previous chapter, I spoke about the need for achieving internal equity. In this one, I moved on to external equity. While both are equally important, sometimes when designing a compensation program, it can be confusing to determine which one is more important. Weighing can be quite the balancing act. For example:

- You might have a role that ranks highly internally because it is a critically strategic role for your company. If you are a software company, for example, then your software architects are probably among the most important roles you have and are, therefore, getting paid at the high end of the market rate, or even over it. However, a hospital that hires a software architect may not weigh the importance of the role as highly, so they'd be more likely to set the job at market rate.
- Another role may be lower in internal hierarchy, but recruiting for those positions is difficult due to a shortage of candidates, while there's simultaneously a high demand for them. Data analysts often fall in this space. While they may not be ranked highly within the corporate structure, you might end up assigning them premium pay because of the external factors.

The above two examples show you how difficult it can be to determine the salary range for a position, even when you are armed with good survey data. In such circumstances, companies must choose between adjusting internal structures to reflect market rates or holding firm to the organization's status quo and risk losing out on recruiting good candidates or losing much-needed employees.

The good news is that you don't have to take any risks. There are strategies to help you balance internal equity with external equity.

- **Use both job evaluation and market data.** The internal value of the job can be the main deciding factor; use market data to define the salary ranges for each of the job's grades.
- **Create flexible pay bands.** You can maintain integrity with your equity by setting wider salary bands for those fast-moving or high-demand roles. Just remember not to put them at outrageous distances.
- **Align your compensation philosophy with business goals.** This concept depends on your company's mission. If you're a startup, then your base salaries may be low due to a lack of funding, even if the market values those positions at a higher rate. And, if you're a non-profit, you may have mission-critical roles where, to attract the right talent, you pay at or above market level, but the administrative positions are below.

Hopefully, what you can see here is that you don't have to choose between internal equity and external equity. You can find a balance that aligns with both how your company values a role and how the market does.

BUILDING A SYSTEM THAT SUPPORTS PAY EQUITY

The whole point of developing (and using) a market-competitive compensation system is so that you can know, for sure, that what you're paying your employees is aligned with what the market at large is paying for similar roles. This is how you'll attract talent, retain that talent, and save your company dollars because you will not be overpaying for roles. By going through this process, you'll create a fair and sustainable compensation system that will be able to evolve as the market does.

A market-competitive compensation system also helps you achieve and maintain pay equity. How?

- It's transparent. By having clearly defined salary ranges, you reduce the possibility that bias will interfere with pay decisions.
- It's consistent. The process of creating standardized benchmarking and job evaluations is replicable across the organization year after year.
- It provides actionable insights. As you go through the market data to do your comparisons and analysis, you'll notice where adjustments need to be made or inequities need to be corrected.

Remember earlier when I said a simple spreadsheet just wouldn't cut it? By now, you can probably see why. Building a sound compensation strategy requires discipline, data, and design. Yes, it's a lot of work. But it will pay off in the long run.

And one of the ways it will pay off is touched on in that last bullet point above: It helps you identify inequities and make adjustments when they are found. The next chapter will continue the discussion around finding inequities as we discuss how to conduct a pay equity analysis.

CHAPTER 5

CONDUCTING A PAY EQUITY ANALYSIS

Now that you're fully versed on what pay equity means and why it's important, it's time to look at how to do a pay equity audit (a.k.a. pay equity analysis). I realize the word "audit" generally has negative associations assigned to it and may even induce fear in some folks. But it is a necessary "evil" that, once completed, may turn out to be a saving grace for you. Because an audit done right will expose the pathway for you to achieve pay equity.

WHY A PAY EQUITY AUDIT MATTERS

An audit is really the only way you'll ever be certain that you are paying your employees fairly and equitably. Through this structured, data-driven process, you'll identify where there are compensation discrepancies between and among people in your organization who are getting paid for comparable work. Likewise, you'll be able to prove you are paying fairly across your positions, regardless of the gender, race, ethnicity, or other protected characteristics of the folks you employ.

A thorough, well-executed pay equity audit will help you:

- Uncover unexplained disparities in pay, which will allow you to address them and get all employees "caught up" with each other.
- Ensure compliance with evolving equal pay and salary transparency laws, saving you from potential fines.
- Demonstrate your commitment to fairness and inclusion, which helps you create a positive corporate culture.
- Proactively address risk before it becomes a legal or reputational issue. Reacting to legal charges for pay disparities puts you behind a potentially expensive eight ball. Nobody enjoys a negative public fallout. It's always best to get out in front of any issues and address them before risking other people exposing inequities within your organization.

Besides all that, and to touch back on what I mentioned at the beginning of this book: Pay equity is just the right thing to do. If your organization values your employees, you will be committed to closing the wage gap. The only way to do that is by conducting regular pay equity audits and making them a business imperative.

STEPS TO CONDUCT A PAY EQUITY AUDIT

You can probably tell I'm a fan of systems and processes. Winging it just doesn't work in every situation. And pay equity isn't something you can assume you've achieved—remember, just about everyone approaches me with "I don't think we have a problem, but…" And it's not something a simple spreadsheet can help you prove. What you need is a process that both demonstrates what equity looks like and provides a way to measure data to determine whether you're aligned with it, and, if not, by how much you are off.

The following steps build out such a process. You'll note it's similar to the Audit–Analyze–Remediate sequence I introduced in Chapter 3 when first discussing how to create internal equity. I stick to that sequence because it's what works. It's what I suggest organizations do, and in fact, it is something I consult on to help them complete.

Each step is integral to the whole process. Each is designed to provide clarity, objectivity, and actionable insights, and they build on the previous step. So do each one, in this order.

Step 1	Define scope and objectives.
Step 2	Collect and clean compensation data.
Step 3	Standardize job groupings.
Step 4	Identify key variables for analysis.
Step 5	Conduct statistical analyses.
Step 6	Interpret results and flag unexplained gaps.
Step 7	Take remedial actions, like pay adjustments.
Step 8	Communicate findings.
Step 9	Ensure legal review.
Step 10	Plan for regular monitoring and audits.

STEP 1: DEFINE THE SCOPE AND OBJECTIVES

To define the scope, ask these clarifying questions:

- Which employees will be included? Are you completing this for all employees in all positions? Or will the focus be a little less broad? Some examples of a narrow scope might be focusing on full-time employees only, those working remotely in a particular state, or those in specific departments.
- Which demographic categories will be examined? Will the audit focus only on potential disparities between genders? Will it look for biases for or against races or ethnicities? Or will you be trying an intersectional combination of gender, race, and ethnicity?
- What pay elements will be reviewed? Here, you're deciding on whether you're sticking to just the base

salaries, expanding to the total cash paid out annually, looking at forms of equity, or including bonuses.

By answering those questions, you'll set clear parameters that define exactly what you're looking for. The next step is to clarify why you are doing the audit by defining your objectives or goals. The following are some questions to ask or ideas to help you get started:

- Is your organization intent on improving its culture? Do you want to increase the level of trust your employees have in you? Are you looking to attract new talent or want to be sure you can retain your top talent? If "yes" to any of these, then your goal is to identify disparities that job-related factors cannot explain. These disparities will most likely reveal unconscious biases you'll need to eradicate within your organization.
- Have you become aware of legislation that affects your organization and that demands pay equity? In this case, your goal would be to comply with the specific regulatory requirements of the state or country.
- Do you want to be sure your company is paying fairly and/or that you're inclusive? Then your goal would be to determine where you currently are so you can establish a benchmark for internal equity progress over time.

It's very possible that what you want is a combination of all of the above. Whatever it is, though, must be identified before you start the process. Otherwise, you risk collecting data that will go unused, because you don't know what to do with it. This is like setting SMART goals versus generalized or vague ones: With vague goals, it's hard to tell when you've reached where you want to be, know how far you need to go, or be able to track your progress mid-process.

Additionally, it's never advisable to have an audit be a one-person show. That is, this isn't something only the HR manager needs to be on board with doing. Complete buy-in of the goals by all company leaders will be required. If some on the leadership team have different goals for the audit, then potentially different approaches, timelines, or resources will be required to complete it. Work together to understand what the organization as a whole is seeking to discover and why.

STEP 2: COLLECT AND CLEAN COMPENSATION DATA

Regardless of your scope and goals, the data you will need to collect for your audit must be clean—meaning that it's been processed to remove incomplete, inaccurate, or inconsistent results—and comprehensive—meaning that it covers everything related to what you're asking for regarding each employee.

The number of different data sets or factors you look into will often depend on the size of your company. The smaller the company, the fewer data sets will be needed. In fact, if you look at too many different aspects for a small company where there may be only one or two people sharing similar roles, you could muddle up your results. Focus on what's most relevant to *your* organization and *your* specific goals for the audit.

Here are some different kinds of data that can be included:

- **Employee demographics.** This includes gender, race, ethnicity, and age, and the intersections among them.
- **Job information.** Here you'll look at the job titles and levels or grades. Keep in mind that compensable factors may be similar across jobs with different titles, so you'll want to go beyond titles and access information in the job descriptions. You'll consider the different departments of your organization. And you'll want to know your employees' FLSA status: Are they exempt or nonexempt from overtime pay?
- **Compensation data.** Your compensation data can be built out of all the ways that you pay your employees. Monetarily, that includes base salary, bonus or commissions, overtime pay, and total cash. Then there are non-wage-based benefits like insurance, 401(k), stock, or equity.
- **Performance and tenure data.** For this, you'll pull information from performance appraisals and evaluations. You'll also want to include seniority, both the

length of time the employee has been with the company and how long they've been in their current role.

- **Other factors.** Again, the compensable factors come into play here. In particular, you may want to review the education, experience, and certifications on record for your employees. And, often relevant for remote workers, you'll consider the geographic locations where they live.

In addition to the above, you may need to refresh your working knowledge about your company's policies as far as compensation practices go. Does every department get the same percentage for a raise? Does everyone get reviewed annually? How are bonuses decided? Are there any other potential differences in any facet as to how those decisions are made regarding paying wages?

STEP 3: STANDARDIZE JOB GROUPINGS

Once you know what you're looking for, why you're looking for it, and you're clear on the kind of data you'll use, it's time to look at your jobs to group apples with apples and oranges with oranges. While identifying different fruits is relatively easy to do at a glance, when it comes to jobs, you'll find here's where those job descriptions really come in handy! A "glance" at a title often isn't enough to put like jobs together properly. Ultimately, you'll be filling buckets with jobs where the employees perform substantially similar work based on job content, not job title.

If the scope of your project is the entire company, don't hesitate to group jobs across different departments. You cannot reach true equity if positions in one department are paid more than those in similar roles in another department. Again, you're looking at the core compensable factors to make your comparisons to group the jobs.

The groups you end up with will be dependent on your organization's structure. Here are some frequent kinds of groupings:

- **Skills and effort.** Those with similar skill levels, or who are required to put in similar effort, can be considered comparable and grouped together. Financial analysts, data analysts, and programmer analysts can all be grouped because their skillsets are similar.
- **Job families.** This is when you form groups based on the jobs' core functions. For example, a "business administration" family of jobs might consist of administrative assistants, office clerks, file clerks, secretarial staff, or receptionists. A tech family might include engineers and technicians.
- **Job grades or pay bands.** If you've created grades or bands through point values or classifications as described in Chapter 4, you could use them for this process.
- **Department or business unit.** This might sound similar to grouping by job families, but it is different. You

could have administrative assistants from many different departments grouped into one family. Here, you could group everyone in the "administrative support" division into a business unit group.

- **Locations and working conditions.** If you have a pay structure that varies depending on whether people are working in-house, in the field, or remotely, then grouping them by locations or working conditions might make sense for your organization.

Your first attempt to create groups may not be the right one. You might want to experiment with different formations until you land on the group structure that works best for your organization. It's important to take the extra step and do it right. Using groups that are too broadly defined may dilute the data so much that you don't end up with a clear answer. On the other hand, too narrow a group's scope may make it hard to tell if there are disparities.

STEP 4: IDENTIFY KEY VARIABLES FOR ANALYSIS

Once you have your job groups figured out, you can look at each one to identify the primary data points that describe your employees to use in your analysis. Those points, which will be your key variables, must be something you can measure or rate in order to do your analysis.

Frequent key variables include:

- **Employee information.** The gender, race, ethnicity, age, sexual orientation, and whether and what kind of disability your employees may have can all be essential for analysis. **Tenure and seniority.** The length of time someone is employed is often a significant contributor to their receiving higher wages.
- **Performance ratings.** When people "exceed expectations" on their performance appraisals, they often get a larger raise percentage than people who "meet expectations" or fall even lower on the scale.
- **Location.** If you have employees working remotely or have in-house workers across multiple geographic locations, where they live and work will influence their wages.

STEP 5: CONDUCT STATISTICAL ANALYSES

Now that you know which jobs you'll be comparing to which, and what factors you'll be focusing on, it's time to do the actual analysis. Here is where you'll use a statistical method to test for pay differences within each group. Software applications such as Excel, R, or Python can help you do this analysis. And there are commercial pay equity platforms specifically designed to streamline this process with efficiency and accuracy.

Whatever you use, there are three common methods for finding disparities:

- **Job groupings.** This is a fairly basic method. You compare the average pay across groups to determine whether there are significant differences.
- **Outlier detection.** After ranking salaries from lowest to highest, you look for individuals whose pay deviates sharply from the others in the group.
- **Regression analysis.** This method is the most complex and precise. It can identify bias and, if any are found, quantify the gap. It can also help determine what factors might have contributed to that gap. For example, if an organization identifies a gender wage gap, is it possible that a particular variable (e.g., difference in experience or education) is also at play? The regression analysis chart below indicates a gender gap.

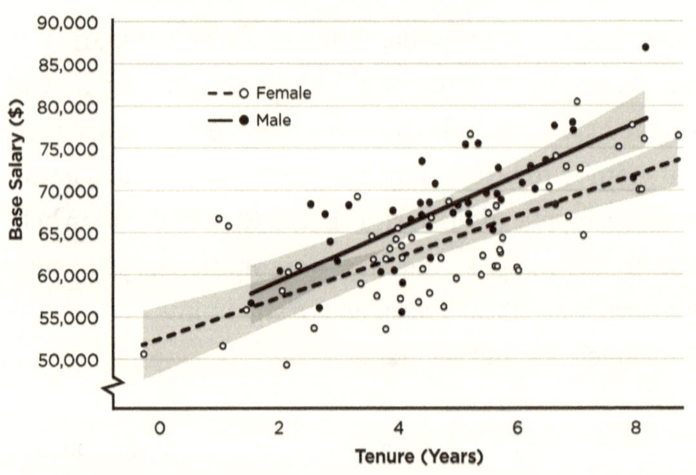

The graph shows there is a positive correlation with tenure, meaning both males and females receive salary increases as their tenure lengthens, which makes sense: More years on the job usually means higher pay.

However, it's also quite clear that a gender pay gap exists. As shown by the darker dots, males consistently have higher base salaries than females, represented by the lighter dots. The two solid lines are regression lines that show the trend of salary increases over time. These lines prove that males have consistently been paid more than their female counterparts. While both lines go up over time, indicating that both genders received similar raise rates, because the male line started at a higher wage, the gap remains and even widens slightly over time.

The confidence bands—the shaded areas flanking the lines show another takeaway. These bands indicate the expected range for most of the data. Notice that there's not much overlap in these bands. That tells us that the pay difference is statistically significant.

In short, the regression analysis graph shows us that men are consistently paid more than women, and the gap between them never closes.

STEP 6: INTERPRET THE RESULTS AND FLAG UNEXPLAINED GAPS

Once you complete your pay analysis, you may notice a range of differences. If you do, I caution you against automatically assuming this is proof of discrimination. Before you can be sure that you have inequities, you'll need to determine whether the pay disparities are explainable or unexplainable.

- Explainable differences can happen for legitimate reasons.
- If a company was small and had only one person as an IT tech for years before the organization ballooned and suddenly had several techs, that original team member's salary may stand out as an outlier, earning much more than the others. That's not a matter of discrimination; it's a matter of tenure.
- Employees attaining degrees or certifications, going through various forms of extra training, or achieving a different role level are all legitimate reasons for them to be paid more than their peers who do not have similar statuses.
- Employees living in different parts of the country, or even different parts of the world, may require vastly different base salaries.
- Unexplained differences are the red flags. These are the gaps that remain after accounting for any legitimate variable. You must look into these gaps and take remedial actions to close them.

STEP 7: TAKE REMEDIAL ACTIONS LIKE PAY ADJUSTMENTS

If you've reviewed the results and identified unexplained differences, then it's time for remediation. You have no choice but to adjust salaries and revise compensation practices where needed. You cannot achieve pay equity if you ignore this step.

How do you make remediations? Well, here are a few strategies:

- **Targeted pay adjustments.** This is probably the simplest and most straightforward approach and is usually all you need to do if you have just a few employees to adjust. Do the math to determine how much to increase the underpaid employee's pay, and start paying them at the higher level.
- **Structural changes.** If you notice that certain roles or groups are consistently underpaid, adjustments to their salary bands may be needed.
- **Policy revisions.** When disparities are discovered, that's a sure sign that the decision-making involved with compensation (starting pay, promotions, and merit increases) needs to be reviewed. You'll want to eliminate the potential for bias interference and inconsistent pay practices, and adjust salaries as needed.

Regardless of how you handle remediating your wage disparities, the important thing is that they never occur again. Your managers, supervisors, HR personnel, and whoever else shares the hot seat for making compensation decisions must be equipped with the tools necessary to make equitable pay decisions.

How you do that can take many forms. Bias training is one of them. Again, no one wants to believe they are discriminating against their employees, but the unconscious nature of bias means that's exactly what they're doing without realizing it. Bias training helps hiring managers become conscious of any unconscious biases when making compensation decisions. Actively promoting diversity and inclusivity measures is another way to reduce the likelihood that pay disparities will become a problem again.

Whatever you decide to do, realize that the compensation decision-makers must also be held accountable to abide by equitable practices moving into the future.

STEP 8: COMMUNICATE FINDINGS

You might feel as if you've done everything necessary by this point—you found the problems and fixed them. What could be next?

Well, what's next is usually not anyone's favorite part of the process. It's time to go transparent and publicly report your findings. While not the easiest messaging you'll ever produce, done well, you'll discover you've actually helped strengthen your trustworthiness in the eyes of your employees.

Some best practices for this step:

- Don't focus on the raw data behind the remediation decisions. Just share your process for discovering there were wage disparities.
- Discuss the actions you took to remediate the gaps.
- Talk about your commitment to maintain pay equity, and back up that commitment by explaining how you have a new process, system, or policy in place not only to prevent wage disparities in the future, but to continue with ongoing improvement of your pay practices.
- What to keep out of your communications is any admittance to being at fault for not having pay equity all along. That's not necessary to discuss and could potentially lead to legal trouble if you start talking about being at fault for any reason.

Here are some examples of effective messaging:

- "As part of our commitment to equitable pay, we conducted a pay analysis and made adjustments to ensure our compensation aligns with our values."
- "We're building a more transparent, inclusive work-

place by reviewing pay practices and holding ourselves accountable."

STEP 9: ENSURE LEGAL REVIEW

Above, I mentioned that you should not admit you were at fault for the pay inequity and suggested obtaining a legal review. Even if you completed your pay equity audit proactively without knowledge or suspicion of wage gaps in your organization, if you didn't consult with an attorney before you started, I suggest you do so immediately afterward. In fact, getting attorneys involved in your process should be part of your remediation strategies.

First, having attorney–client privilege will protect you. By having an attorney provide legal guidance while you conduct your audits, what you find—any disparities, potential proof of discrimination, or any other potentially troublesome result—will be shielded from being part of the discovery process should litigation later arise.

Attorneys will know the laws better than you, so they'll be able to confirm for sure that you are in compliance with federal and state laws. And, whether it's about salary history bans or pay transparency disclosures, some states' requirements can impact your audit findings. The penalties for noncompliance with pay equity laws, as laid out in the Equal Pay Act, Title VII, and numerous state laws, can be hefty. Getting legal advice on how to handle them can help you avoid paying penalties.

A final way attorneys can be of benefit falls under the concept of "good-faith efforts." Massachusetts and other jurisdictions see proactive audits as a demonstration of a good-faith effort to identify and correct pay disparities. As such, by doing them *before* someone else discovers you have a problem is a way to legally protect you from lawsuits after the fact. A good attorney briefed in these laws will be able to ensure that these audits are a strategic approach to protect you from being sued later.

STEP 10: PLAN FOR REGULAR MONITORING AND AUDITS

Final step! Congratulations! I know I just gave you a lot to think about. There's just one more thing to do: Get ready to repeat this process.

I hope you took my earlier suggestion to document how you conducted your audit, so you'll have a ready-to-use process to do it on a regular basis. Sure, it may be tempting to think that once you have remedied the disparities and put in new systems, processes, and policies, you have nothing to worry about in the future. But complacency is seldom a good strategy. Laws change, job descriptions change, different unconscious biases can sneak in...any number of things can happen to create inequity in a formerly equitable organization.

I suggest you set a recurring cadence to reevaluate your pay equity status annually (I'll revisit this in Chapter 12). By making it part of your yearly compensation review cycle, you'll never have to be reactive and fix a problem after the fact. Even better, you'll be proving your commitment to maintain equity.

Your pay equity audit is more than a statistical exercise to "make good" on inconsistent pay practices. It's a powerful tool for cultural change. When organizations take the time to investigate and address pay disparities, they prove to their employees that they are, in fact, a company people are happy to work for. A company that's trustworthy, credible, and transparent.

CHAPTER 6

THE ROLE OF TRANSPARENCY IN CLOSING THE WAGE GAP

The use of the word "transparency" increased in books by over 72 percent between 1990 and 2022.[18] Why? Many believe it's because the internet enabled us to gather and share data with ease, which created a means to hold governments and businesses accountable for telling the truth. And what better way to prove you are doing what you say you are doing with your resources and funds than to be transparent with your data?

---

18   Google Books Ngram Viewer, s.v. "transparency," accessed March 2, 2026, https://books.google.com/ngrams/ graph?content=transparency&year_start=1800&year_end=2022&corpus=en&smoothing=3.

THE CASE FOR PAY TRANSPARENCY: TRUST AND ACCOUNTABILITY

I'm still surprised whenever I discover a company that has banned its employees from discussing wages. Though I guess I shouldn't be. According to a recent survey, about half of all workers in the United States say their companies discourage it, and many say they will be punished or disciplined in some way if they are caught talking about their wages or the pay of anyone in the company.[19]

My surprised reaction is because discouraging the topic is technically illegal for most employers and has been since the National Labor Relations Act was passed in 1935. However, because no serious disciplinary actions were ever invoked for violating that law, for several decades, companies frequently did their best to keep compensation a confidential subject.

But times change. As transparency became more embraced as a good policy for companies, as noted in Chapter 2, more state and federal legislation included things like requiring employers to post salary ranges in job listings, and to provide accurate information when employees asked to see pay bands. Those laws have also banned companies from disciplining or retaliating against employees who openly discuss wages. In short, pay secrecy is discouraged.

---

19 "Pay Secrecy and Wage Discrimination," Institute for Women's Policy Research, accessed March 2, 2026, https://iwpr.org/pay-secrecy-and-wage-discrimination-2/.

I applaud the move to be more open to compensation discussions for a number of reasons. First, the best way to prevent inequality and inequity is through transparency. When all employees know how much they are being paid in comparison to their peers, it's next to impossible to continue wage disparities. And, to go beyond the numbers, when the rationale behind compensation decisions is known and freely discussed, employees feel respected; they know they are being treated fairly, so they feel valued. This leads to better engagement with their jobs and better satisfaction at work. They can *trust* that their employer is doing the best they can for them. So now companies can use transparency as a way to signal they are a fair and equitable organization.

But transparency doesn't mean having your payroll open and on display. Nor does it require broadcasting the salaries of every person employed within your organization. Best practices include providing your employees with the information they need to understand and trust your compensation system.

LEVELS OF TRANSPARENCY: WHAT TO SHARE AND WITH WHOM

Deciding what to share and with whom requires thought and deliberation. While to a certain degree transparency is mandated, your organization has some control over the information they disclose and to whom they disclose it. You need to have a strategy for how you handle compensation information, one that you abide by with consistency.

For most organizations, that strategy will have levels of transparency; think of them like levels of secrecy within a government. Not everyone needs to have access to top-secret stuff. The following is a spectrum of transparency levels to help you think about what you will share, who you'll share it with, and the impact you can expect from such transparency.

PHILOSOPHICAL TRANSPARENCY

- **What it includes:** You'll share your organization's compensation philosophy. Remember, this is about the strategy your organization uses to determine pay—base wages, benefits, etc.—along with the factors influencing those amounts, and how fairness is ensured. This also includes how you pay compared to the market: below market rate, at market rate, or above market rate.
- **Audience:** All employees.
- **Impact:** Notice you're not sharing individual pay data here. The purpose of this level of transparency is to solidify the trust your employees have in your intentions. They need to know you're doing the best you can for them, and they can rely on you to continue to do so.

- **What it includes:** Providing a framework that shows how you use criteria like market benchmarking, performance evaluations, employee experience, or education, etc., to make compensation decisions.
- **Audience:** All employees and job candidates.
- **Impact:** This builds trust because you're proving your decisions are made with logic and reason, not just by whims or possibly with favoritism. It also emphasizes how fair your compensation practices are.

RANGE TRANSPARENCY

- **What it includes:** Depending on which state you live in, this might be legally mandated. You will disclose the hourly or salary ranges, as well as a description of benefits or other forms of compensation, in all job postings, even when they may be listings for promotions or internal roles.
- **Audience:** Applicants and employees being considered for new roles or promotions.
- **Impact:** This prevents pay gaps from starting because it puts an end to negotiation biases, which means there is consistency across offers to all candidates.

- **What it includes:** Responding to employees who ask for details related to their salary bands with the dollar spread of their position. It also includes explaining why they fall where they fall within that band, and how they can progress to the next pay level.
- **Audience:** Individual employees.
- **Impact:** The impact of this level of transparency is more for the employee than for the organization. But, as with all the levels discussed here, it helps build trust in the company. When employees are given this information, they feel empowered and even inspired, as they can understand their growth path as well as identify opportunities for advancement.

FULL TRANSPARENCY

- **What it includes:** As the name suggests, this is where you share everything. This includes salary ranges for individuals, pay scales, and information on how salaries are determined. This information is published openly with nothing obscured.
- **Audience:** Often public (as seen with government positions), or it can be kept internal but made available to all employees.
- **Impact:** This is a very bold step that not all companies can or should take. However, if you have a solid system, one you've audited, and you're clear in how you present

the information so it's neither confusing nor open to misinterpretation, then it's one of the best things you can do for accountability and to earn the trust of your employees.

Even if full transparency is a goal for your organization, ease into it. Be eager to adopt transparency measures that are in alignment with state and federal mandates, but work your way through the levels strategically. Any misstep can potentially backfire and impede the trust and accountability you're trying to grow. Proceed deliberately and allow transparency to evolve in ways that are aligned with your company values.

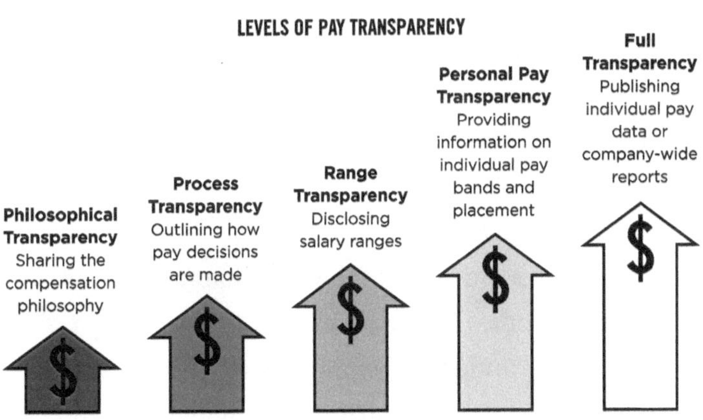

COMMUNICATING PAY PRACTICES EFFECTIVELY

Were you triggered at any point while reading about the levels of transparency? Were you thinking something like,

"Sure, this sounds great! I love the idea, but what's going to happen after we share this information? Will an employee think we should have been paying them more all along and try to sue us?"

That's a common reaction I receive. However, besides getting legal counsel as I suggested, that's why you use this process the way I explain it. Even if you are curious about gender equity, that's not where you start the process.

Here's how you do it:

- You start by looking at how everyone in the organization is paid relative to the market (Chapter 4), then build salary ranges in alignment with the market.
- At that point, you can audit your compensation records, look at all your employees to see how they are paid against the market first, then see how they are paid against the salary ranges.
- Next, you do an equity analysis (Chapter 5) to look for gender or other biased disparities in similar jobs.
- You'll have an idea of who is low for the market, who is paid low in their salary range, and who is paid low compared to their counterparts. You take that data, compile it to create remediation for everyone, and then you make a *market adjustment.*
- You can sit down with every employee who will experience a compensation increase, and say, "We measured

the marketplace (maybe even hired a consultant like me) and looked at what we were paying. We wanted to be transparent and build ranges. Now we want to make sure you are paid appropriately for both the market and for our internal ranges. Therefore, we are giving you this compensation increase adjustment. Next year, we'll look at it all again and see if another adjustment is necessary."

You are making a market adjustment for everyone, which will also fix any other disparities in the process. The state and federal government just want you to identify pay issues and fix them, so you will be in compliance. Your employees will be happy to know they are paid fairly at market rate. So, if you stick to this process and get legal counsel to ensure you're in compliance, all that's left is learning how to properly communicate the information you're being transparent about.

Transparency without context can cause you problems. If you skip explaining why you're sharing compensation information, or you are not careful about *how* you explain it, you risk your message being misinterpreted by your employees or having them draw the wrong conclusions about why you did what you did. So, *effective* communication is essential.

Here are a few key strategies for communicating pay practices clearly and consistently:

1. CLARIFY YOUR COMPENSATION PHILOSOPHY

What does your company value? What are the reasons behind your pay decisions? Those are two questions your employees will want answered. They are also two questions you'll answer when you describe your compensation philosophy. Your compensation philosophy will also reflect your commitment to maintaining equity, staying in alignment with the market, and any other guiding principles.

You'll communicate this philosophy in your onboarding materials, employee handbooks, and in internal portals. It should also be part of any career conversations you have.

2. TRAIN MANAGERS TO TALK ABOUT PAY

Most employees will go to the person they report to when they want to talk about their pay or compensation practices. Usually, that means their managers, who seldom feel equipped to answer their questions. To make the conversation more comfortable for managers and empower them to say the right things, provide them with:

- Talking points about how compensation decisions are made by your organization.
- Training on how to have these potentially sensitive conversations in a respectful and clear way.
- Guidance on what can and cannot be shared.

Always remember that your managers are on the front lines for reinforcing trust in the organization. They are likewise positioned to contribute to any confusion, which could lead to increasing angst or frustration among your teams. Keep your managers informed with both accurate information and the skills to convey it.

Here is an example of an emailed communication for your managers:

> Supporting a Culture of Pay Equity at [Company Name]
>
> Our company is making a commitment to pay equity.
>
> While there may be a legal requirement for equity, our primary goal goes deeper than that. Pay equity is a reflection of our core values. We believe all employees should be treated with integrity and respect, and they should be paid fairly.
>
> Because you are a manager, you are in direct contact with the people on your team on a regular, if not daily, basis. You are often seen as the face of this organization and play an important part in the creation of an inclusive, credible, and fair company culture.
>
> In that capacity, you are a point person to answer compensation-related questions. We are counting on you to:

- Become more than familiar with our compensation policy. Know it, understand it, and follow its tenets. Be prepared to answer any and all pay-related questions about the philosophy and pay ranges.
- Be consistent when defining the criteria that support hiring, promotion, and other pay-related decisions.
- Be objective. Always have documented evidence to back up all staffing recommendations.
- Be an active participant in HR training sessions, especially those focused on pay equity issues and practices.
- Be transparent and respectful when communicating pay decisions and information.

Additionally, following are best practices we encourage you to adopt:

- When making job offers, use the established pay ranges and do not take into consideration any salary history of the candidate.
- All performance reviews should have clear performance metrics to use as the basis for increases and bonuses.
- Promotion criteria should never be a mystery. Always ensure it is well-documented and used equitably.
- Be open to listening to the concerns of all employees and don't hesitate to elevate concerns or issues to the appropriate channels.

To support your efforts to be the face of our compensation

philosophy and answer questions, we have created the following resources:

- Compensation FAQs
- Training materials on how pay equity is determined
- Designated compensation experts on the HR team
- Wage grades, salary ranges, and clear guides defining all internal job levels

We appreciate your willingness to be a proactive team player as you take on the necessary communication your leadership role requires. It's critical that everyone genuinely trusts our compensation process and systems. Thank you for always being transparent, fair, and consistent with every compensation conversation you have with our employees.

Should you need extra help or guidance, reach out to [HR contact email] with any questions.

3. PROVIDE TOOLS AND RESOURCES

Being transparent includes making your compensation information easy for your employees to find whenever they want to. The following information is what they should always be able to access with ease:

- Their salary range and their position within it
- The various pathways for promotion

- Avenues for salary growth
- FAQs that answer questions related to everything about compensation, including how raises, bonuses, and equity are determined

4. ACKNOWLEDGE AND EXPLAIN ADJUSTMENTS

If a pay equity audit leads to salary adjustments, frame the conversation so you're explaining that the organization is proactive about being fair. It's that simple. For example:

"As we completed our annual compensation review, we realized there were a few opportunities for us to improve alignment with the market rates and our pay equity goals. So, we've made adjustments where appropriate."

5. BE TRANSPARENT ABOUT TRANSPARENCY

While the levels of transparency define who should receive what information, note that there's no need to release it all at once. Let your employees know about your plans gradually, and keep them informed about your plans. For example, you could tell them, "Right now, we're sharing our salary ranges with all employees and candidates, and within the next year, we expect to roll out our full compensation philosophy to the public."

Why would you do that? Well, it builds credibility, especially when you follow through on your promises. And you're also explaining to everyone that transparency is an evolving process that takes consideration and time.

TRANSPARENCY AS A CULTURAL SHIFT

You're probably starting to get the feeling that transparency isn't just a tactic to employ, but that it's an actual cultural shift. As with any change to a corporate culture, it requires courage to start it, commitment to follow through on it, and a willingness to be held accountable. Yeah, it's a lot. But, it's so worth it.

Organizations that embrace transparency:

- Discover that their employees trust them more.
- Find that their employees are more engaged with their jobs and the company at large.
- Have fewer pay complaints.
- Are less at risk for litigation.
- Develop a strong reputation for being fair and equitable employers.
- Define clearer pathways for career development and growth for their employees.

To get back to what I started this chapter with, the desire and expectations for companies to be transparent about their pay practices are growing. Nowadays, it's commonplace for employees to expect honesty and fairness regarding their compensation, which means transparency is just no longer optional. Aside from that, it's one of the best tools to ensure we close the wage gap and create pay equity.

CHAPTER 7

ORGANIZATIONAL STRATEGIES TO CLOSE THE WAGE GAP

With so many discussions on processes in this book, I understand if you think all that's required to close the wage gap is a little data analysis and making adjustments so you're legally compliant. While that is a huge part of what's required, there's actually quite a bit more to think about. The ultimate goal isn't just to achieve equity; it is to create an organization that puts equity into action.

What does that look like? How does putting "equity into action" show up in the corporate world on the day-to-day level? Well, as discussed earlier, it will be evident in your organization's culture. When equitable practices become integral to your identity as a company, they'll be entrenched in your systems, strategies, and communications. Fairness will be operationalized. Inclusiveness becomes a reflexive consideration in every talent conversation or decision, whether that's about recruiting, providing pathways of promotion, or simple annual raises.

Changes will happen across the organization's strategies that make pay equity easily sustainable because it becomes the norm. This chapter explores how to evolve operational strategies to incorporate equity. In particular, I'll focus on how to set equity goals and KPIs, how to embed equity into your compensation philosophy, and how to install and follow through on inclusive practices.

SETTING MEASURABLE EQUITY GOALS AND KPIS

Every business professional has heard it dozens, if not hundreds, of times: *What gets measured gets managed*. And the platitude holds true with pay equity. If you want to make it a strategic goal for your organization, the only way to ensure you meet it is, as with every goal, you make it measurable by using key performance indicators (KPIs).

I can hear you now: "But wait! Didn't I just do a bunch of measuring over the past three chapters?" Yes, you did. That was to discover what you need to do to achieve pay equity in compensation. What I'm talking about here are equity goals that influence how you operate as a business from this moment onward.

ESTABLISHING EQUITY GOALS

So, let's think about this: What types of equity goals should your organization make? Several answers will likely show up when you do your audit and may resemble the following scenarios.

- Did you discover a surprising number of unexplained gender and racial pay gaps? If so, then your goal could be to close them within a designated time frame.
- Did you notice that salary offers had no parameters and seemed almost haphazard? Then your goal could be to ensure that all offers will be made within your (new) established pay ranges for each role.
- Did it become apparent that there were few, if any, underrepresented groups in leadership roles? Then a goal here would be to be more inclusive and increase their numbers.

Once you have an idea of what your equity goals are, you'll want to frame them as SMART goals, because, again, to use something we've all been told numerous times, that's the best way to reach your goals. In case you need a refresher, a SMART goal is a specific, measurable, achievable, relevant, and time-bound objective. Defining each of those characteristics for your goal will help provide a way for your organization to have a clear direction and a way to hold itself accountable as it makes progress on the goal.

An example of a SMART equity goal is: For all roles where we have more than ten employees, we'll reduce unexplained wage gaps to less than 3 percent by the fourth quarter.

- **It's specific:** Reducing roles with ten-plus employees with wage gaps by 3 percent
- **It's measurable:** You can measure both the number of wage gaps and the percentage of the gap size.
- **It's achievable:** You have a process to do an analysis and make remediations.
- **It's relevant:** It has a significant and demonstrable impact on your company's ability to be in legal compliance.
- **It's time-bound:** By the fourth quarter of the year, you'll be done.

DEFINING KPIS TO TRACK PROGRESS

With any goal, but especially with SMART ones, you'll need to identify KPIs for tracking your progress and knowing when you've hit your goal. Your unique situation may present you with specific KPIs, but here are the most frequently used for pay equity goals:

- The percentage of benchmarked roles that are aligned with current market wage rates.
- What is the percentage of employees who are within the targeted pay ranges for their grades?
- The percentage of new hires and promoted employees who have wages aligned with your compensation guidelines.
- The frequency of your pay equity audits.
- The outcomes of pay equity audits.
- Pay gap ratios by gender, race, and intersectional groups.

Whatever KPIs you assign, by creating a dashboard to track them, you can get real-time insight as you work toward the SMART goal. You'll have an easier ability to discern where your problem areas are while still in the process, and you can hold your leaders accountable.

Here's an example of a dashboard built around percentage metrics. At a glance, you can see where you are in alignment with market rates, pay range targets, and new hire/promotion compliance, as well as how you're doing regarding the resolution of audit findings.

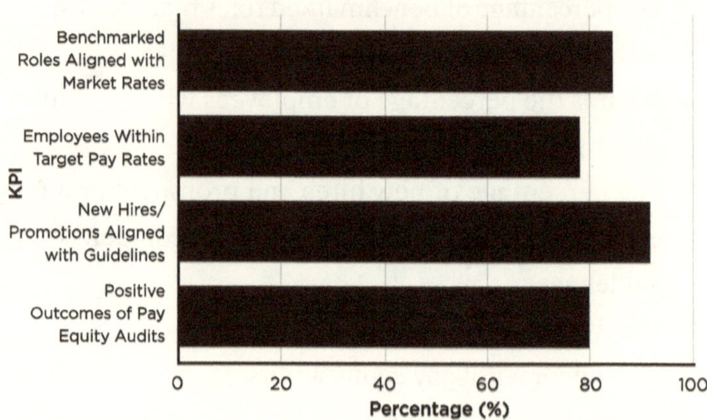

The following table displays common KPIs and target recommendations:

Key Performance Indicator (KPI)	Target/Benchmark
Gender Pay Gap (Median percent)	Less than 5 percent gap
Racial/Ethnic Pay Gap (Median percent)	Less than 5 percent gap
Percent of Employees Within Pay Range	95 percent or higher
Percent of Salary Offers Within Pay Range	100 percent
Number of Roles Benchmarked to Market	100 percent of core roles
Percent of Managers Trained on Pay Equity	100 percent
Number of Pay Equity Audits Conducted Annually	At least one per year
Percent of Pay Adjustments Completed Post-Audit	100 percent
Promotion Rate by Gender and Race	Equal rates across demographic groups
Engagement Survey—Pay Fairness Score	75 percent plus agreement

How you talk about your goals and what, exactly, you share is entirely up to your organization. There are benefits to publicly disclosing your equity targets. Doing so can strengthen accountability and build trust with employees, investors, and customers.

However, organizations that want to get their feet under them and feel their approach is the right one and strong, may want to only share internally. Again, transparency isn't an all-or-nothing switch you flip. You can gradually move into sharing more and broadening your audience as you become more confident with the process and your results.

The main idea, whether you share internally or externally, is that your communication is consistent in subject and scope and that you follow through on doing what you say you're going to do.

EMBEDDING EQUITY INTO COMPENSATION PHILOSOPHY

I spoke about compensation philosophies earlier; they're basically the guiding ideology behind why you pay your employees and how you pay them. So, if equity is truly something your company aims to embrace, it needs to be an integral part of your compensation philosophy. Otherwise, you risk the day-to-day wage or salary decisions made without any consideration of equity.

WHAT A COMPENSATION PHILOSOPHY SHOULD INCLUDE

The following list helps you build or revamp your compensation philosophy so equity is a primary focus.

- Affirm your commitment to achieving (if you're not quite there yet) or maintaining fair and equitable pay across all roles within your organization.
- Define the parameters you use to balance internal equity with external competitiveness (see Chapter 4).
- Explain how you determined the pay ranges and the rationale behind bonuses and incentives.
- Ensure that your employees know your compensation practices are bias-free, and that race, gender, or other demographics are never taken into consideration.

While all that sounds as if I'm expecting you to write a five-paragraph essay, really, it can be summed up within a sentence or two. For example: "Here at [insert company name], we believe all employees should be compensated fairly. To that end, we are committed to paying everyone a fair wage that is aligned with market rates and based on their individual performance and internal job value. We will review our compensation data annually to maintain equity for all."

Of course, once you communicate how equity is a fundamental part of your compensation philosophy, you have to back up your talk by walking it, which means consistent implementation. To that end:

- Everyone involved with hiring decisions (your HR teams, managers, etc.) must be trained in the philosophy well enough to incorporate it into their hiring, review, and promotion decisions.
- Every compensation decision-making process should have "equity checkpoints" to ensure equity is included as part of the process.
- Create a compensation committee, equity council, or some form of an oversight structure responsible for ensuring that fairness and consistency exist throughout the company.

Securing equity into your compensation philosophy, then creating actionable methods to ensure your organization follows through on what that philosophy mandates, is how you proactively prevent compensation issues. It is how you can save your company from taking a reactive approach to fix things after the fact.

I gave you a brief snippet of how to include equity in the verbiage of your compensation philosophy. Below is a template showing how that statement can be contained within a full compensation philosophy.

[Company Name] Compensation Philosophy

Here at [insert company name], we believe all employees should be compensated fairly. To that end, we are committed to paying everyone a fair wage aligned with market rates and based on their individual performance and internal job value. We will review our compensation data annually to maintain equity for all.

Our compensation practices are designed to:

- **Safeguard internal equity.** We evaluate roles based on their relative value within the company.
- **Maintain our external competitiveness.** Our pay practices are benchmarked against appropriate market data.
- **Exemplify appreciation.** We recognize and reward individual performance, contributions, and potential.
- **Create a culture of pay equity.** We embrace a system that allows us to minimize and prevent pay disparities across gender, race, and other demographic characteristics.

The key principles of this compensation philosophy include:

- **Market-based compensation.** Regarding base pay and total compensation, our goal is always to be aligned with market medians while allowing flexibility based on skillsets, experience, and business needs.

- **Pay-for-performance.** We use merit increases and incentive programs to reward high-performing employees based on clearly defined goals and achievements.
- **Transparency.** Our commitment to pay equity is exemplified in our willingness to openly communicate our compensation philosophy and salary structures.
- **Legal compliance.** We remain in full compliance with all federal, state, and local compensation laws. Additionally, we conduct pay equity analyses and compensation reviews on an annual basis to ensure we stay in compliance and that our compensation practices evolve in parallel with our business strategy and employee needs.

INCLUSIVE HIRING, PROMOTION, AND PAY PRACTICES

The third strategy I suggest companies use to ensure the wage gap is closed and stays closed is to embrace inclusion. Where diversity encourages hiring a diverse group of people to work in your organization, inclusion is what you concentrate on after they are hired. It's about the actions you take that let *all* the people in your company know they are respected, valued, and empowered to expand in and beyond their current positions.

Because inclusion informs how people come on board, get promoted within, and receive raises, it can be a major contributing factor to wage gaps. So, if you are intent on closing any wage gaps, including everything already mentioned in this book, you must look at your compensation systems through an inclusive lens to evaluate whether changes must be made for the sake of equity.

Let's look at how that happens in the hiring, promoting, and pay practices systems.

INCLUSIVE HIRING

- **Have an interview structure.** While everyone appreciates a relaxed, "get to know you" interview, it's best to stick with consistent questions and scoring rubrics in a structured format to reduce bias. You can still be friendly!
- **No salary history.** This was mentioned before, but it bears repeating. Just because someone was underpaid at their last job doesn't mean they should be underpaid in your organization.
- **Disclose salary ranges.** Even if your state does not mandate including the salary ranges in job postings, do it anyway to provide equal negotiating power for all who apply.
- **Embrace diversity.** Ensure the candidates you consider for open positions, as well as people in the hiring chairs, are diverse. This will help deter groupthink while also increasing representation.

- **Regularly audit.** Collect the data related to promotion raises and analyze it to uncover potential gender, race, or other demographic gaps.
- **Clarify promotion criteria.** How and why people are chosen for promotion should have clearly defined parameters and a rationale that are also consistently applied across areas of the organization.
- **Mentor and sponsor.** Create programs for underrepresented employees and encourage participation to ensure everyone has access to advancement opportunities.
- **Promote on consistent schedules.** Different teams or departments may take longer than others before advancing employees from one role to another. Track all advancements to guarantee consistency across your organization.

FAIR AND CONSISTENT PAY PRACTICES

- **Merit increases.** "Merit," when it comes to employee performance, means that a person did something specific to subsequently earn a raise. To help determine the amount of the raise and keep it fair across the company, merit increases should have performance-based criteria and not be left up to the manager's discretion.
- **Offer guidelines.** If you do not post the salary range with the position, then create and use internal guide-

lines so candidates are offered pay that aligns with their internal peers.

- **Annual pay equity audits.** See Chapter 5. Conduct these annually and always make remedial adjustments for any gaps you discover.
- **Transparent communication.** All conversations and written communications about benefits, bonuses, or promotions must be clear, concise, and cogent, as well as presented in a way that all employees can understand.

I hope it's clear that once pay equity is achieved, it's not possible to truly maintain it unless you incorporate it into your compensation philosophy and ensure equity covers the full talent life cycle. All decisions regarding pay, from the time a position is posted as open to hiring, to promoting, to offering bonuses, and to any other pay considerations impact how equitable your company is. You must fully embrace the concept and take intentional action to get equity established as part of your business norm.

EQUITY REQUIRES INTENTIONAL ACTION

As with most organizational change, achieving equity isn't a matter of thinking about what it's like to have equity; you have to take intentional action. When a company does something with intention, all involved are completely, consciously aware of the purpose behind what's happening, why it's happening, and the consequences of it happening.

That deep connection to the action takes on more meaning and helps the change become part of the DNA of the organization.

When a company can close the wage gap through intentional actions, they show up in the world:

- as bold goal setters and getters, unafraid to measure progress,
- with equity embedded into their compensation philosophy and systems, and
- embodying a thriving, inclusive culture that offers everyone pathways for hiring, development, and advancement.

Yes, taking intentional action toward creating equity requires courage. It calls on you to be clear about what you're doing and why, and consistent as you make progress on your goals. It's hard work, but the reward is a stronger and fairer workplace, with a committed talent force.

CHAPTER 8

CREATING A CULTURE OF PAY EQUITY IN THE WORKPLACE

In Chapter 3, when I wrote about the necessity of embedding pay equity into your corporate culture, I emphasized that achieving pay equity is simply not enough. You must create a system to maintain it. The thing is, culture and systems have a symbiotic relationship: Without a culture supporting and encouraging the system, you risk equity not being valued enough to prioritize, and without the system supporting the culture, you risk equity silently fading away.

In this chapter, I'm going to talk about how to strengthen both your systems and your culture. I'll go a little deeper into how your organization can cultivate a culture where pay equity is so thoroughly integrated into your values and policies (i.e., your systems) that it's part of your norm. Some of this may be familiar, as I've touched on these concepts in different parts of the book already. Here, I'm pulling them all together, so you can see their intersections and expand on them.

There are three ways you can control the narrative to ensure pay equity becomes part of your company culture and systems:

- Get leadership to commit to the cause
- Train managers as frontline advocates
- Build trust with employees through transparency and engagement.

LEADERSHIP COMMITMENT AND ACCOUNTABILITY

Leadership always creates a cascade effect. If leadership performs subpar at the top, the organization below will deteriorate. The opposite is also true. If leadership is great at the top, the entire company below them will develop into their fullest capacities, and the values and priorities the leader embraces will be what everyone under them will embrace.

When leaders champion pay equity in their actions as well as their words, the trickle-down effect becomes obvious as we discover everyone at every level doing likewise. By making decisions with pay equity clearly in mind, modeling behavior that supports treating everyone with fairness, and being outspoken about how they value pay equity, leaders create a cascade effect that influences their entire team to do the same.

Walking the pay equity talk doesn't have to be difficult, but it has to be intentional. Here are several strategies to help leadership get pay equity embedded in the company culture.

SET THE TONE FROM THE TOP

At the executive level, traditional forms of communication are great opportunities to bring up pay equity. Take advantage of them through these methods.

- Be public about it. Encourage your marketing or PR teams to incorporate your commitment to pay equity into press releases, your branding materials on social media, and websites, and at every opportunity where the information has a natural fit.
- Periodically review your mission statement and all materials where you express your corporate values. You can include or update your determination to treat all employees fairly in those important cultural assets.
- Make it a regularly featured talking point. Bring your organization's commitment to pay equity into your annual reports if you create them. If you don't, con-

sider releasing reports that detail your equity goals, the progress you have made already, and what you are committed to doing in the future. Acknowledge gaps honestly and frame solutions as part of a long-term commitment.

It's also important that you are *seen* as the decision-makers behind and proponents for pay equity, too, so you cannot rely solely on information people will read when you're not in the same room with them. In addition to "official" language and communications, executives need to embrace equity to the point where they can feel comfortable and confident talking about it. Any time an employee asks a question related to equity, whether that's in the break room or in a meeting, speak openly and honestly about it, because it builds more trust than any corporate communication with your name on it.

MAKE PAY EQUITY A STRATEGIC PRIORITY

We've all been on the receiving end of bad customer service from an employee who works for an organization that prides itself on having great customer service. That kind of thing happens when the communications say one thing and the company strategy says something else. Similar situations can happen with pay equity if the organization doesn't have a strategy in place. That's why it's so important to integrate pay equity into the way you run your business.

If equity audits are an annual or even semiannual requirement, and KPIs are tracked in a dashboard, you have a good start for making equity a strategic priority. You can build on that through these ideas:

- Ensure your organization includes pay equity initiatives as part of your goals for talent recruitment or retention. Make pay equity outcomes one of the measurable goals to reward leadership performance.
- Think about how you can include pay equity in your employee development strategies. Use your audit results to determine who is being paid inequitably, then create the necessary training or pathways to help those employees develop the skills or background required for promotions or raises.
- Train hiring managers and HR on ways to mitigate unconscious bias in hiring, performance evaluations, and promotion decisions (more on this below).
- Include pay equity and compensation rationale in the education provided in onboarding materials for all new hires.

Additionally, anyone in a compensation, decision-making capacity within the organization should be empowered and enabled to openly ask questions about your compensation philosophy and the audit results. This includes members of your board, all executives, the people in management and leadership positions, and all HR personnel. Going further, they should know it's expected of them to ask questions and even challenge processes to ensure ongoing progress and maintenance of pay equity.

ESTABLISH GOVERNANCE AND OVERSIGHT

Both embedding pay equity into your culture and creating strategies to support it will benefit from having some form of oversight to ensure those tactics have a consistent impact. No organization is static. Meaning, there is a constant influx of personnel as new employees come on board, and a shift happens while current employees make cross-functional moves, receive promotions, or leave the organization. That state of fluidity makes it easy for the emphasis on pay equity to wane. So, consider creating a form of governance to keep the focus on equity. Ways to do that include:

- Have dedicated people on a pay equity council or task force who are responsible for analyzing audit results and following up on recommendations to correct found disparities.
- Establish reporting cycles with deliverables based on reviewing audit results and remediation plans as part of performance expectations for leadership or compensation decision-makers.
- Create channels to make cross-functional communication and collaboration easy among HR, legal, finance, and leadership.

- Include equity reviews as a regular item of discussion in all compensation committee meetings.

Implementing structured accountability methods ensures that equity data remains transparent. Additionally, overseeing remediation efforts will be crucial for maintaining pay equity within your organization.

TRAINING MANAGERS ON EQUITABLE PAY PRACTICES

When discussing ways to make pay equity a strategic priority, I touched on the concept of training leadership on equitable pay practices. Here, I'm encouraging you to go a level deeper into your organization and consider your managers' roles in pay equity. Yes, leadership sets the vision, the company goals, and often the strategies to achieve those goals, but it's usually the managers in the trenches who follow through on what needs to be done. They're the ones making the final hiring decisions, recommending raises, signing off on performance reviews, and suggesting promotions. They also frequently serve as the face of your organization. They are the point person fielding direct questions from employees about their pay and the compensation practices of the company. As such, they are the daily stewards of your pay equity goals and strategies.

If your managers are not thoroughly educated on your compensation philosophy and informed of your equity efforts, whatever you're trying to achieve at the level of the entire company could be accidentally undone on the management level. To empower your managers to support your equity efforts, they must have the knowledge and tools, the resources, and someone monitoring their engagement.

EQUIP MANAGERS WITH KNOWLEDGE AND TOOLS

Pay equity should be an essential topic in all management training, whether you're promoting someone from within the organization or bringing someone in from outside. Additionally, it should be included in all personal development you offer and reemphasized on quarterly or annual business reviews.

What do you talk about? Here are some pointers.

- **An overview of the company's compensation philosophy.** For newly installed managers, you'll discuss why you pay what you pay, and how you determine raises and promotions. Regularly, you'll review those points and train on any changes that may be necessary.
- **Guidance on how pay decisions are made and what criteria to use.** Share the salary ranges and why they are set, and train on recognizing unconscious bias in action.
- **Dos and don'ts of equitable hiring and promotion**

practices. Insist on pay transparency and enforcing pay band parameters. Again, reinforce unconscious bias training.

- **Case studies or role-playing scenarios to navigate tough conversations.** How you do this will be tailored to your compensation philosophy. The benefits of this point are twofold. One: Your managers will feel more confident and empowered to answer employee questions about pay. Two: Those tough conversations, when handled well, do a beautiful job of proving your organization's commitment to transparency.

As with most training, compensation and pay equity coaching isn't a one-and-done event. The way equity manifests in your organization will evolve over time. Make sure your managers are always up to date.

PROVIDE RESOURCES FOR PAY CONVERSATIONS

If you skip any of the previous points, make sure it's not the last one about handling tough conversations. Remember, your managers are often on the front lines of your company's operations. Any time they avoid a conversation because they don't feel confident in their ability to have the discussion, or they totally mishandle it because they are unprepared, can be a risk for your organization. Whether that shows up as employees being disgruntled because they see it as a lack of transparency or, possibly worse, they become misinformed about their wages, that is not an outcome any organization wants or needs. To help your managers find their footing and accurately talk about wages and pay equity, give them what they need, which includes:

- Compensation talking points and FAQs.
- A direct and clear channel for seeking answers when they do not have them.
- Templates for performance reviews that enable unbiased evaluations and salary bands to guide pay increases and bonus awards.

One of the best ways to build trust in your organization while also reinforcing the fairness of your compensation program is through well-informed managers. Giving them what they need to succeed in their role will support your organization's equity efforts.

MONITOR MANAGER IMPACT

As with any form of training, you'll never know if the people on the receiving end understand what they've learned well enough to implement it, or whether what you're training is working, unless you follow it up by monitoring the impact of it. The way to do that here, regarding equipping your managers, is to track the outcomes your teams or departments are achieving to identify disparities in how compensation decisions are applied. Key questions to ask or data points to look for can be found in the following:

- Are your audit reports showing evidence that certain managers consistently award lower raises or bonuses to specific demographic groups? If so, then training on unconscious biases and reinforcement of salary bands must happen.
- Looking at the promotion rates across all teams, are they aligned? Or do some teams have much higher or lower rates than others? If you have a problem here, look at the criteria each department uses for evaluations.
- Is there evidence that salary offers are consistent across similar roles? If they're not, salary ranges need to be reinforced, and unconscious biases may also need to be addressed.

Data will always be your friend when it comes to pay equity (and just about everything else!). Your audit results will provide more information than just answering, "Are we paying fairly?" Use those numbers to hold your management accountable for their role in maintaining pay equity.

EMPLOYEE ENGAGEMENT AND TRUST-BUILDING

Leadership and management buy-in isn't enough to create a culture where pay equity is so entrenched that it can thrive. Employees must be on board with what you're doing too. And they will if they believe the systems you're creating are fair. Even better, they'll be eager to support your efforts if they know they have a voice in what you're doing. Encouraging their belief and trust in you requires good communication, which enables their involvement in the process, in celebrating your progress, and showing them the positive impact of pay equity every day.

COMMUNICATE EARLY AND OFTEN

Good communicators do not wait until people need to know something before they tell them. They realize that communicating well ahead of the "need to know" phase increases the odds of the messages being received and understood. They also know, especially in this age of abundant content, that their messages must be recommunicated and updated on a regular basis.

When you couple early and frequent outreaches with transparency, the result is confidence that the messages are true and trustworthy. So, what should you communicate? Well, pretty much everything related to your equity efforts, such as:

- Explain why you're doing pay equity audits. Yes, tell them about legal compliance, but make that secondary. Be sure to use this opportunity to express the organization's commitment to pay equity and being fair to all employees.

- Tell them how you're remediating pay disparities. Describe the actions you're taking.
- Let all employees know what they can expect. Talk about your equity goals, the systems you're putting in place to maintain equity, and describe the governance and oversight measures you're taking.
- Create pathways and opportunities to open the dialogue about compensation. Give your employees a way to ask questions and provide feedback.

As with all communication, avoid jargon. Use plain, clear, and concise language to avoid misunderstandings or risking the appearance of not being transparent.

INVOLVE EMPLOYEES IN THE PROCESS

Something that might get lost in the pay equity conversation is that pay equity isn't something done *to* or *for* employees; it's something that should be done *with* them. This is their livelihood, after all. They should be included in the conversations, and their input should be included in the pay decisions. Here are ways you can do that.

- Create employee advisory groups tasked with providing feedback on compensation changes and the compensation philosophy.
- Regularly conduct anonymous surveys to get a feel for how fair your employees believe your wages and you are.

- Hold townhall-type listening sessions specifically focused on compensation and career advancement.

Note the above points do not suggest you should let your employees dictate how much you're going to pay them. What I am suggesting is your employees should feel empowered to talk to you about wages and salaries, knowing you are listening and interested. When employees feel heard and involved, they are more likely to trust the outcomes, even if they don't always agree with every detail.

CELEBRATE PROGRESS

Be patient. Creating changes in a corporate culture can take time. To offset feeling impatient, celebrate the milestones you hit along the way. For example:

- When you close a pay gap in a department or job family.
- When you launch new training or transparency initiatives.
- When engagement surveys verify you've improved employee opinions on how fair you are.

There will be plenty more opportunities to celebrate your progress as you move along. Keep your eye open for these opportunities to reinforce both your commitment to pay equity and your employees' support of it.

FROM POLICY TO CULTURE: EMBEDDING EQUITY EVERY DAY

Once you create a culture of pay equity, fairness embedded into every level of your organization will be just one of many positive results. Others will include more clarity about how jobs are defined and raises are awarded. You will discover more cohesion among teams, and strong trust will grow within your organization. Your entire workforce will become more committed than ever to your organization.

So yes, while learning how to have honest conversations about potentially sensitive concepts, making hard decisions, and holding people accountable is seldom easy or fun, just know the rewards will pay off exponentially. Like gears in a well-oiled machine, the ideas will keep your corporate culture fully functional and operating effectively.

CHAPTER 9

THE ROLE OF TECHNOLOGY IN ACHIEVING PAY EQUITY

As with everything else in business (and life), technology transforms the ways we can identify, remediate, and prevent pay disparities. There are a few programs you can use to do your audit and track how well you're progressing toward your pay equity goals. You can take advantage of the tech world by exploring how to use predictive analytics and artificial intelligence.

If you're in the HR field, you may already know many tech tools on the market that uncover biases and program equity into your compensation decision-making. This chapter takes you a step further and discusses how you can use HR analytics, AI, benchmarking platforms, and automation to create smarter and more compliant pay systems.

USING HR ANALYTICS AND AI FOR PAY EQUITY MONITORING

I can't tell you how many times a client responded to me in shock and embarrassment after their audit revealed pay disparities. They didn't understand how the disparity was even possible in the first place. When they learn it's been there sometimes for many years, they can't figure out why no one noticed.

I already spoke about the most common cause for disparities to begin: Different groups ask for different starting salaries. Posting wage ranges and sticking to them fixes that issue. So the question then becomes, "Why do they stay hidden?" The answer is that most organizations haven't invested in the right tools to discover the gaps.

Those tools exist. In particular, HR analytics and AI can identify, address, and prevent future compensation disparities. Let's look at how they work.

THE POWER OF PEOPLE ANALYTICS

Modern HR systems can use statistical and data mining techniques across your entire compensation program and for all employees throughout their tenure with your organization. From hiring wage decisions to performance and promotion raises, these tools can assess the fairness of your compensation practices. They can quickly expose the patterns and correlations that would take you hours or even days to do manually.

Some findings include:

- **Gaps in starting salaries.** You will know if there are specific demographic groups who are consistently being hired below the midpoint of the pay grade, as well as who is consistently hired at the highest point of the grade.
- **Merit increase variances.** If women, certain races, or ethnic groups get smaller merit increases on average, that will be exposed.
- **Ever-widening pay gaps.** Remember that graph in Chapter 5? There we saw how the pay gap only grew wider during an eight-year time span. That didn't have to happen and would have been found much more quickly if HR analytics had been used to monitor the company systems.

I could continue this list by talking about how these tools can also help with benchmarking compensation, tracking trends over time, or analyzing pay drivers like tenure or performance to justify pay raises. I'll do that soon; for now, I hope you get my point that these tools can save you a significant amount of time and money, which is great. But they can help you even more when you bring in the power of AI.

PREDICTIVE AND PRESCRIPTIVE AI

"Predictive AI" has achieved buzzword status. Just about everyone in the business world has heard it and is intrigued by the concept (though, admittedly, several are a little fearful as well). Basically, predictive AI is what you use to forecast or model likely events in the future.

The phrase "prescriptive AI" is less tossed about. Its superpowers lie in its ability to take the forecasting that predictive AI does and, through data and statistics, recommend actions to improve the outcome of whatever you're looking at. For pay equity:

- Predictive AI can show you where you'll likely find future pay gaps. Maybe that would be in fast-growing departments or for those roles where you have a substantial pay grade or salary range.
- Prescriptive AI takes that forecast and recommends creating starting salary ranges based on internal equity and market data for the jobs in that team. For example, it could create a system to ensure pay is consistent within a broad salary range by setting levels based on education, experience, special skills brought to the job, or other factors.

Hopefully, you can see how predictive and prescriptive AI can help tighten up your compensation practices to prevent disparities. However, it's still AI we're talking about. That means it will function as programmed and will only be as fair as its algorithms. You must make sure you are using a system that does not have bias built in and that it will be transparent about its methods. Otherwise, you'll be working with machines that act just like humans.

Additionally, data quality remains an issue. Start with clean data; otherwise, you'll get lackluster results that won't be helpful.

PRIVACY AND GOVERNANCE

We always have to remember when we do anything with the data in our pay or compensation records that we're working with highly sensitive information. It's a big responsibility we should never take lightly, and we should always do our best to keep personnel information confidential. Through the use of data privacy protocols, governance frameworks, and cross-functional oversight, you can feel confident you are taking the necessary steps to protect your employees' data.

Data privacy protocols include encryption, role-based access controls, and adherence to regulations intended to ensure confidentiality. Those kinds of practices safeguard sensitive employee information and decrease the likelihood of data breaches or leaks.

Securing your data is a significant first step, but it's not enough for complete protection. You'll want some kind of oversight to ensure your tools are working ethically and in compliance with the legal requirements your company abides by. That's where having governance frameworks comes into play. You can create governance frameworks to define the criteria for selecting your programs and how your AI will be informed.

You have the tech part buttoned up. But you'll still have humans working in the departments who will rely on the HR analytics and AI tools. You still need cross-functional oversight among HR, your legal team, and other leaders involved in your pay equity efforts. By bringing them together, you can be sure your pay equity efforts are legally sound yet operationally practical, while aligning with your corporate values.

As someone who's been doing equity audits and creating remediation efforts for years, I think having AI and analytical tools is pretty exciting. Used and applied thoughtfully, they can help make the shift from being reactive to proactively tackling any equity issues that may arise much more easily.

TECHNOLOGY FOR ONGOING COMPENSATION BENCHMARKING

When I spoke about developing a market-competitive compensation program in Chapter 4, you thought it looked like a long and difficult process. And it can be. Hence, most companies do it just once a year. However, by using technology, you can take it from being a manual exercise to an ongoing process that is updating with real-time compensation data. That means, on top of saving you time and energy, you have an avenue for always being in alignment with market rates.

DIGITAL BENCHMARKING PLATFORMS

Using digital benchmarking platforms will make it easier for you to:

- Access updated market data from trusted sources. These platforms are programmed to regularly pull data from systems like HRIS (Human Resources Information Systems), compensation surveys, government databases, and data-sharing networks.
- Look at and compare the responsibilities, skills, and requirements of positions to benchmark jobs based on content and scope, versus sticking to using job titles.
- After accessing and aggregating data from external sources like HRIS, these platforms can be programmed to automatically filter out irrelevant information and

segment the relevant information into categories before comparing them with what's going on in your organization.

I think it's pretty clear how automation can save you the time, energy, and aggravation you'd otherwise have to invest in doing similar market benchmarking. But, not to sound like a used car salesman, *there's more!* The platforms often include dashboards and visualizations that make it easy to determine where your job positions stand in comparison with similar ones in the market. And you can set these systems up to automatically alert you whenever your salaries drift out of range with market trends.

There's just one more thing left for you to do: integrate the benchmarking findings into your pay cycles.

INTEGRATING BENCHMARKING INTO PAY CYCLES

Why do you need to do this? Because it's how your organization will remain competitive with similar companies. Because benchmarking platforms are continually pulling up-to-date information, you will always be informed of what's fair and equitable. This means you can:

- Help retain and attract top talent. If your salary ranges are updated frequently, as these platforms easily allow, then you will always be competitive. Your current employees will know you're paying them fairly, and you'll look attractive to potential new candidates.

- Have appropriate budgets based on current data so merit increases can be maximized while staying within pay bands.
- Have a solid rationale for salary-hiring decisions as well as for increases related to promotions.

An underlying benefit is the real-time data that digital benchmarking platforms provide is what will help prevent the lag, the opening crack in fairness that allows inequities to grow over time. These tools provide you with an easy way to ensure everyone within your organization is paid fairly every day of the year.

AUTOMATION TO REDUCE HUMAN BIAS IN PAY DECISIONS

So far in this chapter, my focus has been on the things that are relatively easy to see and quantify for pay equity: numbers. But that solves only part of the problem with pay disparities. The other part is a bit harder to quantify, and that is human bias.

Fortunately, automating systems can eliminate human bias in your pay decisions. Granted, we must always remember that humans build these automated systems based on their human behavior and thoughts. Therefore, no system currently on the market completely lacks subjectivity. However, by all means, they are much less biased than humans-in-the-flesh, which makes them better-informed tools for pay decisions.

Automated systems provide frameworks and programs that can create structure for compensation processes. By using them, managers and HR salary decision-makers will be at a reduced risk of inconsistent pay practices or possibly being influenced by favoritism. Here are a few to consider.

- **Salary offer configurators.** These tools can help you customize job pay offers based on the market value of the position and the candidate's credentials, skills, experience, and location. There's no need to ask about prior salary, and because these tools integrate with your internal data, there's no risk of paying them outside of your salary ranges.
- **Merit increase calculators.** When it's time to recommend raises, these calculators automatically factor in any predefined criteria your organization has set for raises (like performance ratings) and the pay bands for the job. In that way, they allow for increases without you risking them going out of salary range.
- **Promotion justification templates.** These templates work because they are structured frameworks that

require specific, standardized input. They'll have areas where you can enter the employees' achievements and key performance indicators that prove whether they are ready for a promotion. You can also highlight skills, experience, and even leadership qualities. In short, these templates allow you to connect performance to their promotion objectively.

While these tools do not work with hard data like numbers, you can take what could easily be subjective factors in pay decisions and make them objective. By doing so, they reduce variability in wages, which means reduced potential for disparity due to unconscious biases. They promote fairness, and they provide a paper trail of sorts...an electronic paper trail as you'll have the documentation to back up your commitment to maintaining pay equity.

REAL-TIME SALARY RANGE VALIDATION

I can't emphasize enough how helpful having real-time pay data available is! We can set up alerts or notifications whenever we're about to pay someone out of the approved range for their position, or when it's inconsistent with their peers. This real-time validation works at the moment of making the first salary offer, at each performance review, and at any time in between. So, if there's unconscious bias happening, it gets checked at the door.

TRANSPARENCY AND AUDIT TRAILS

By automating every aspect of your compensation decisions, you create a historical record. Every offer you make, every increase you allow, every change in wages for any reason is recorded, time-stamped, and even reviewed for compliance. Earlier, I said this "paper trail" would be evidence of your commitment to equity, which is great for supporting your corporate culture. But it has other value too.

This historical record can be a linchpin for transparency. When employees ask about salary ranges or information on how you justify your pay decisions, you can use these records to back you up. When you're being audited or need to provide documentation for legal review, you'll feel confident knowing these records accurately portray your equitable actions and results.

TECHNOLOGY AS AN ENABLER—NOT A REPLACEMENT

I hope this chapter doesn't give you the impression you can leave everything related to making compensation decisions up to your computer systems. While yes, tech can play a powerful role in your company, please always see it as an enabler of pay equity. Meaning, it will *help* you achieve and maintain pay equity; it cannot do everything. You and your human judgment will still be needed to provide leadership, create strategies, and even be empathetic with your employees. That will show up in the day-to-day as you:

- Become the voice of reason, logic, and empathy behind creating your compensation philosophy.
- Provide oversight to ensure that whatever automated tools your organization uses are in alignment with your mission, values, culture, and goals.
- Keep context in mind as you interpret the data the tools give you. Behind the data, there will always be real people with real experiences that sometimes don't get accurately interpreted through the lens of computational analysis. You have a responsibility to protect the interests of your employees, which may sometimes mean questioning what the data shows.

So, yes! Embrace the technology that's available to use in your compensation strategies. But always remember it will not be the only driving force making pay decisions. The humans using the machines should remain at the helm when you're talking about the livelihoods of your employees. Use this tech wisely, as an enabler, not as a replacement for you or your leadership. Done right, it will help you become more efficient and accurate as you scale.

CHAPTER 10

EMPOWERING EMPLOYEES TO ADVOCATE FOR EQUAL PAY

Something I've yet to talk about in this book is the employee's role in achieving and maintaining equity. You may find it odd that I'd have a chapter devoted to that role and may even question what the employees have to do with anything. After all, it's the employer who creates the pay bands, the employer who does the hiring and promoting, and it's definitely the employer who would pay the fines if they were found to be out of legal compliance. So where does the employee fit in this equation?

While you, the employer, have the lion's share of the work involved to close the wage gap and keep it closed, your employees have a part to play too. That part includes taking an active interest in understanding their rights and finding the courage to advocate for themselves and their fellow coworkers. Many companies may want their employees to do both of those things, and there might also be some anxiety around the concept. There is so much misinformation on the internet that can quickly spread to break rooms...it might seem like a risk to have fully informed employees.

The good news is you can be the ultimate source for your employees. You can empower them by promoting education, open dialogue, and peer-driven support networks. By getting involved, you can be sure your employees are getting the right information they need.

EDUCATING EMPLOYEES ABOUT THEIR RIGHTS AND COMPENSATION

A side benefit of empowering your employees to know their rights is that you'll strengthen your culture. By providing the knowledge they need to self-advocate, you build their trust in you. And when they understand how their pay is determined, they'll be less likely to believe rumors or suspect you're not paying them a fair salary.

So, you'll want to begin there, by teaching them the basics of your compensation philosophy.

TEACH THE BASICS OF COMPENSATION

If you've gone through the steps outlined in this book to discover and address any pay equity issues you might have, and you've established a compensation philosophy, then you're already armed with what you need to teach your employees about your compensation practices. Remember, you're not providing every detail here. Your goal is to demystify how your organization makes decisions regarding pay.

You'll want to:

- Describe your company's compensation structures. This means explaining how the parameters are set for salary bands, defining what goes into job groupings, and dissecting bonus plans to show how they are fairly determined.
- Clarify how each compensable factor is considered and weighed when making wage decisions.
- Be open about how market data and internal equity are weighed to determine salary bands.

How you provide this education is entirely up to you. A best practice is to start at the beginning of the employee life cycle by incorporating it into your onboarding materials. You'll immediately instill trust in your organization. Then, for employees already hired, you can maintain the transparency by having educational sessions after each annual equity audit or as part of the compensation practices review. You can also refer to it during the employee appraisal process and create a compensation FAQ on an internal employee portal.

PROMOTE LEGAL RIGHTS AND PROTECTIONS

Most employees are aware of certain basic laws that protect them as workers. Just about everyone knows the Equal Employment Opportunity (EEO) law prevents discrimination when making hiring decisions. Many will have an idea about how the Occupational Safety and Health Association (OSHA) helps guarantee their workplaces are as physically healthy as possible. But few realize the laws that protect them for their pay.

That means you can provide them with the opportunity to learn more about those protections. By doing so, again, you'll strengthen your culture. You'll build trust. And you'll help your employees know they can be confident that you are doing what you need to do to pay them fairly.

Here are some ways you can help your employees know their legal rights:

- Provide summaries of relevant laws like the Equal Pay Act, Title VII, and whatever your state's salary and transparency statutes say. Refer to Chapter 2 for talking points.

- When you discuss your compensation philosophy and pay structures, be sure your employees know they always have the right to talk about their pay with other employees without fear of retaliation.
- As part of your regularly scheduled trainings and new-hire onboarding, hold "Know Your Rights" workshops to keep this information up-to-date for them.

The more your employees understand your pay decision-making strategies and are informed about their legal rights, the more informed and empowered they will feel. It will encourage them to be self-advocates if the need arises. But wanting to self-advocate only goes so far if the person doesn't have the know-how or courage to follow through with it, which is another place where you can help them.

ENCOURAGE SELF-ADVOCACY SKILLS

Even the most confident employees feel intimidated or at least unsettled when speaking up about their pay. The fear of retaliation is real and has been fueled by popular news stories, books, and movies. Such apprehension doesn't have to be necessary. Healthy work cultures strive to prevent it and encourage their employees to feel comfortable and confident during any pay-related conversations.

Courage always comes before confidence, and preparation fuels courage. So, to help your employees reach a level of confidence to self-advocate, you can offer training or share resources with them that:

- Prepares them for compensation conversations with managers. You could give them a script or checklist of typical talking points or a list of FAQs regarding pay decisions they can use as prompts.
- Provides baseline info that prompts questions about salary ranges and growth opportunities. Arm your employees with your compensation philosophy or other guidelines related to pay bands, promotions, and raises, along with self-assessment tools. This will give them a jumping-off point where they can compare their perceived performance with management's assessment, then ask questions about bridging that gap.
- Teaches how to negotiate respectfully and effectively, without relying on prior salary as a benchmark. Negotiation skills are seldom innate and must be taught. Consider adding such training to your other scheduled teaching opportunities.

To empower your employees to feel comfortable and confident enough to ask pay-related questions, your goal should always be to normalize the subject. Gone are the days of treating salary discussions as taboo. Let's encourage these necessary conversations that are essential to maintaining pay equity.

CREATING SAFE SPACES FOR DIALOGUE ABOUT PAY

Talking about pay or asking questions related to the company's compensation strategies is always easier for employees when they feel safe while doing so. Anytime they fear they'll create conflict or friction, or they believe they'll be negatively judged or retaliated against, employees will hesitate to come forward with their concerns or questions.

Being open and honest to educate them about their rights and encouraging discourse goes a long way toward instilling a sense of safety around the topic. However, organizations can take this a step further by creating psychological safety and structured opportunities for open dialogue. Let's look at ways to do that.

NORMALIZE CONVERSATIONS ABOUT PAY

You begin normalizing conversations about pay at the level of organizational culture. That means you're mindful of the words you use to encourage employees to broach the subject. Using inclusive language like, "We welcome your questions and feedback on how we manage pay" has a totally different ring than, "See the FAQs for any pay-related issues." The first example encourages employees to actively initiate compensation conversations, and the second one lets them know you don't have the time to answer anything that hasn't already been thought of.

Such inclusive language shouldn't remain at the corporate communications level, though; it should be embraced by everyone in HR, management, and leadership. Additionally, as part of their commitment to "walking the talk" of equity, as described in Chapter 8, management and leadership must adopt and maintain an open and fair mindset for all compensation discussions. Dismissing attempts to hold these conversations or rushing through them will only discourage employees from trying to talk about their concerns at a later time, or worse, encourage them to grumble in the break room about how "no one wants to talk about salaries around here."

A third avenue you can take to normalize pay discussions is to be open about recognizing and even rewarding transparency in leadership. If that first equity audit exposes disparities, use it as an opportunity to talk frankly and honestly about pay. Or, when you learn of someone in management taking the time to share the why behind a promotion decision, acknowledge how that was the right thing to do. Whether you do it when feeling like you have egg on your face or in a celebratory manner, by taking advantage of opportunities to discuss pay or wages openly, you will establish the topic as a safe thing to discuss.

A final strategy you can take to normalize these conversations involves facilitating peer-learning events. You can consider hosting things like:

- "Ask Me Anything" sessions where HR or management are ready to answer any questions about pay equity.
- Lunch-and-learns for employees to get a full understanding of how job levels and pay ranges are determined.
- Panel discussions, town halls, or fireside chats where employees who've successfully advocated for themselves take questions from an audience of their peers.

These are all about creating comfortable, relaxed environments to have open discussions. Because they are *not* for debates or challenges, they encourage respect and listening as they normalize the topic of compensation. But just because something is "normal" doesn't mean everyone wants to talk about it all the time. So, you'll also want to create confidential pathways.

OFFER CONFIDENTIAL SUPPORT CHANNELS

The topic of compensation is not one that everyone will want to talk about in public. That's why I suggest companies create other methods to make it easy for employees to discuss wages or raise pay-related concerns. You can do that by offering anonymous surveys or suggestion forms, for example, or by having dedicated staff in HR be the primary contact for all pay-equity questions. Another strategy is to have anyone in a position who has input on or control over compensation decisions hold office hours specifically for "drive-by" conversations at the designated times.

Regardless of how you encourage your employees, you'll know you've been effective when you realize they comfortably speak up whenever they have a pay question or concern, which is ultimately what you want. Without having trusted pathways to get information and share concerns, you risk your employees becoming so upset that they broadcast their concerns on social media or other external channels, or (possibly worse) file legal complaints.

By embedding these conversations into the everyday culture, by normalizing them, you support your employees as they develop their individual self-advocacy skills. And you build on that by introducing them to the concept of shared advocacy, which means you need to support employee resource groups.

SUPPORTING EMPLOYEE RESOURCE GROUPS AND PEER NETWORKS

Employee resource groups (ERGs) are formed within companies by volunteer employees. Usually, they are based on some type of shared background, interest, or some other commonality and are recognized and supported by the company. Similarly, peer networks form when employees connect to share information and best practices. Both groups can also be powerful vehicles for advocacy, especially when you provide them with resources to help their members.

Treat these groups as partners, because they are; they can and will help shape the culture of your organization. Support them by offering mentorship programs where their members can learn leadership skills or be prepared for promotions. Provide them with training in negotiation skills. And give them a safe space to meet, share their challenges, and practice self-advocacy.

Additionally, give your ERGs and peer networks access to:

- Compensation decision-makers who can answer questions when the groups meet.
- Anonymized data from equity audits showing where you are, and the progress you're making to achieve equity.
- Budgeted funds so they can bring in external speakers for workshops or conduct peer-to-peer learning sessions.

Another way you can show your support for ERGs and peer networks is to celebrate their advocacy wins. Make an effort to acknowledge and share success stories from their efforts to advocate for fair play. This could show up as simply as congratulating an employee who asked for and received a role reclassification or pay review. Or it could be on a larger scale, where an entire team is lauded because they provided feedback that subsequently caused the compensation structure for the team to be updated.

A TWO-WAY STREET TO EQUITY

What I hope I've made apparent so far in this chapter is that when you empower your employees, you give them the opportunity to play an integral role in developing and maintaining your company's equity. Yes, audits and data analysis provide a structure and method of achieving equity, but it's your employees who are at the heart of making equity a lasting cultural change through their conversations, their willingness to be educated, and their ability to advocate.

To help jump-start your employees' active participation in pay equity within your company, use the following as a basic template that you can customize for your company's unique perspective and place in the market. Realize there are a few bullet points that will need to be tweaked according to your state's legal mandates.

KNOW YOUR RIGHTS: PAY EQUITY AND TRANSPARENCY

Every employee in this company has legal rights related to fair pay, transparency, and workplace equity. We feel it's important that you are aware of and understand these rights and that you feel empowered to advocate for yourself or others if you ever feel these rights are not being honored. To support both those goals, we're supplying the foundational information below.

- The Equal Pay for Equal Work Act (Equal Pay Act of 1963) safeguards your right to receive equal pay for the work you do that is substantially equal to the work others are doing, regardless of your gender. "Equal work" is not determined by job titles, but by the skills, effort, responsibility, and working environment necessary to fulfill the position's requirements.

- The Protection Against Pay Discrimination Act (Title VII of the Civil Rights Act of 1964) prevents employers from discriminating against anyone based on race, color, religion, sex, or national origin for compensation. That includes all forms of compensation: starting salary, promotional increases, bonuses, etc.

- The National Labor Relations Act (NLRA) secures your right to discuss wages and working conditions with fellow employees. This act protects you by forbidding employers from disciplining or retaliating against anyone who engages in such conversations.

- Our state pay transparency laws require employers to be transparent regarding salary ranges, which means including those ranges in job postings or providing them upon an employee's request.

Tips for Advocating

- If you're unsure about your position's pay range, ask your manager or HR what it is and how it was defined.

- Before having conversations about your compensation, get prepared with the data and information that goes into our decisions regarding your salary. This will include:
- Your job description highlighting your responsibilities.
- A list of achievements or recognitions you've received.
- The market value for your position. You may need to ask HR for this salary range.
- Be active with your peer networks or employee resource groups. Attend their meetings and take advantage of any support or training they offer.
- If you ever suspect there are pay disparities or pay discrimination happening at our company, report it immediately to HR or your state labor agency.

Always remember, it's your right to ask questions about your compensation and to advocate for being treated in a fair manner.

If you have any questions, please don't hesitate to reach out to [Your Company HR Contact] or visit your state's labor department website.

There is yet another way your employees can help you achieve your equity goals. And this one is often a favorite among employers: using pay for performance, which I'll talk about next.

CHAPTER 11

USING PAY FOR PERFORMANCE TO ACHIEVE EQUAL PAY

Pay for performance is probably the most intuitive, familiar, and widely used compensation strategy around. Why? For two reasons. The first is because it's a simple process: Reward your employees by paying them based on their performance. The second is because it drives results. Employees will often work harder and get better results if they know their income will increase because of it.

Done right, pay for performance can also be a method of aligning the individual contributions of each worker with your organization's overall success. The keywords in that sentence are "done right." Because if you're not carefully managing your pay-for-performance processes, you can unintentionally create or exacerbate pay gaps that will undermine your equity efforts. This often occurs when rewards are calculated in inconsistent ways across different teams or departments within your organization. It can also be a result of bias influencing performance evaluations.

To prevent both negative potentials, this chapter will cover how you can leverage performance-based pay systems to support pay equity and not undermine your efforts to create it. You'll discover that by intentionally aligning pay-for-performance strategies with equitable practices, you'll create a powerful tool that will help close (and keep closed) the wage gap while also driving performance and promoting accountability.

DESIGNING EQUITABLE PERFORMANCE-BASED COMPENSATION SYSTEMS

If you've been following what I've written so far in this book, then the first step in creating your pay-for-performance system should already be done: You'll already have defined salary ranges with midpoints for each position. Before you can develop an equitable pay-for-performance system, those ranges need to be established. Your performance evaluations will be what you use to determine where in the salary ranges your employees will be compensated.

Next up, you'll want to create a clear structure that rewards outcomes fairly across all employees and groups. This structure should also remove any ambiguity and minimize the risk subjectivity influencing any decisions. Subjectivity is also known as that thing that allows bias to seep into decision-making. To prevent that, you'll want a clear set of principles to back up and support the entire process by encouraging objectivity.

PRINCIPLES OF AN EQUITABLE PAY-FOR-PERFORMANCE SYSTEM

To promote fairness as much as reward performance, pay-for-performance systems must:

- **Align rewards with measurable outcomes.** When you can link pay increases, bonuses, or promotions to measurable outcomes, you reduce the potential for unconscious bias and the risk of employees being rewarded because they are known well by or are good friends with the manager.
- **Be consistent across roles and functions.** Rewarding performance should be something that happens across all employees in the company. If you reward only the executives or key, high-performing teams, you will create pay gaps that will grow over time. Everyone who gets a performance appraisal or review can be eligible for pay-for-performance, so if one person gets it, everyone should.

- **Ensure visibility and understanding.** Transparency is your number one tool for obtaining trust and respect from your employees. For pay-for-performance systems, every employee needs to know how the performance ratings are determined, what data is used, how their performance impacts their compensation, and who the pay decision-makers are.
- **Include both individual and team components.** All positions in your company ultimately impact the overall team or corporate goals in some way. Including metrics that measure their contribution to those goals will provide a way to create a balanced reward that recognizes individual excellence and collaborative success, which will reduce inequities in recognition.

STRUCTURING THE COMPENSATION ELEMENTS

Once the underlying principles are established to support your pay-for-performance system, you can look at the components to include in it. Those components and their purposes are shown in the table below.

Component	Purpose
Base Pay	Because the base pay is benchmarked to the external market and aligned with internal equity, it is the anchor that ensures your employees are fairly compensated prior to any promotional raise. It serves as the floor that sets the framework for performance-based rewards.
Merit Increases	These tie individual performance to contributions. It is a way for companies to reward employees who meet or exceed performance expectations. They are also how organizations can show their appreciation in a way that is based on objective compensable factors.
Short-Term Incentives	By providing annual bonuses, commissions, or project-based rewards to individuals or teams for achieving goals, you drive performance and reinforce accountability.
Long-Term Incentives	By rewarding continued performance over an extended period of time through retention bonuses or milestone rewards, you can align employees' interests with your organization's objectives and retain top talent.

Of course, each component should be looked at through an equity lens, which means they are based on objective data and applied fairly to all employees. No one should be disproportionately at an advantage or disadvantage compared to other groups of people. This brings me to a discussion on how to avoid bias during performance evaluations.

AVOIDING BIAS IN PERFORMANCE EVALUATIONS AND REWARDS

So far in this chapter, I've used the word "objective" or "objectivity" four times. Considering there has been only one subsection for the chapter, that's a pretty high usage rate. The reason I've stressed it is because objectivity requires data, facts, and metrics: things that preclude bias. So, to create an equitable performance-based pay system, you need to be objective.

When you lose the ability to be objective, you risk equity. It's that simple.

But being objective is hard. Even when you rely on facts and data, bias can unintentionally influence decisions and cause inequities. Knowing what to watch for can help prevent that. Following are the most common forms of bias during performance reviews.

COMMON SOURCES OF BIAS IN PERFORMANCE REVIEWS

1. **Affinity bias.** This happens when managers rate employees more favorably because they have something in common: a shared background, a hobby, they belong to the same social club or religious institution, they have the same health condition, etc. Anything that can create a strong sense of camaraderie can lead a manager to feel they are closer to someone or that they understand them in a deeper way than they do others, which can influence their pay or promotion decisions.
2. **Gender/racial stereotyping.** Even though treating women and people of color equally is the root of all our equity laws, the possibility still exists that they may be

evaluated under a more rigorous focus or even seen as not leadership material.

3. **Leniency/severity bias.** This bias can affect all the employees on a team or under a particular manager. It happens when a manager tends to rate everyone either too high or too low, which shows up in your equity audit as anomalies in the relative job values.

4. **Recency bias.** Some might call this a long-term memory problem. This kind of bias happens when, shortly before the performance appraisal, something occurs that makes an employee look far better or worse than average. If management isn't careful, the recent events can overshadow the employee's performance throughout the evaluation period.

5. **Halo/horns effect.** This bias usually occurs when there is not enough for the manager to base their decisions on, so they use what little they have. If all they know is a positive trait (halo), perhaps the person is always cheerful or willing to help a fellow employee, then they give them high ratings despite their actual job performance. If it's a relatively negative trait (horn), perhaps the employee is an introvert and the manager misinterprets that as being standoffish, then the employee may receive very low job ratings.

Again, let me stress, I don't believe any manager willingly thinks in a biased way. No one wants to think they would ever intentionally be unfair to their employees. Unfortunately, it's the inherent nature of biases being unconscious that makes it tricky to avoid them.

Because the topic of bias has such a negative reputation, it is often an uncomfortable one for managers or anyone in a decision-making seat to talk about, and it can be difficult to fix. Bias awareness training will be helpful here, but again, having a strong factual, objective basis to build your case for promotions and raises will ultimately be what will justify all payroll decisions.

In addition to bias-awareness training, you can reduce bias in performance evaluations by focusing on equity-driven practices.

EQUITY-DRIVEN PERFORMANCE MANAGEMENT PRACTICES

The time will come when you will have to prove why you chose the pay rate you chose. Among the first things a high-performing employee will ask you is, "How do I get paid at the top?" While tenure is one way for that to happen, their performance can speed things up. The person to explain how that acceleration will be possible will most likely be a manager.

Whoever the decision-maker is, sitting down to justify the pay rate one by one and face-to-face with employees can be scary, especially if they don't have the expertise to figure out the numbers. But, by doing some analysis, managers and decision-makers can come up with an inarguable number that will defend their decision—a number that is not factored through bias. Here are a few ways for them to do that:

- **Use structured, competency-based rating scales.** Evaluating vaguely described job attributes like "communication skills" can encourage subjectivity. Instead, break down what you're reviewing into observable and specific behaviors you can rate. Keeping with the communication skills example, this could be active listening (Do they summarize the main points of discussions? Do they ask clarifying questions?), public speaking (Do they deliver presentations with confidence? Do they engage with the audience?), or even conflict resolution (Do they negotiate effectively? Do they remain calm in difficult conversations?).
- **Train managers to recognize and mitigate bias.** This should include training on how to be aware of unconscious bias, to provide fair feedback, and to exhibit inclusive leadership.
- **Involve multiple reviewers or calibration panels.** When you have more than one person in the reviewing process, particularly when it's a diverse group, you minimize the risk of bias. Having the same groups preside over all evaluations also supports efforts to maintain relative job values.

- **Use data to detect anomalies.** Your equity audit will identify if there are particular demographic groups who are consistently rated lower or higher than others despite having similar output.
- **Document evaluations rigorously.** Using examples and evidence to justify ratings will actually make your managers more comfortable with the process. Having facts and figures to back them up can be a real confidence booster.

MONITORING OUTCOMES TO ENSURE FAIRNESS AND IMPACT

By following everything outlined in this chapter, you'll be set up with a pay-for-performance system that will support your efforts to maintain equity. But, as with everything that requires human input and interaction, there's no guarantee that inequities will never slip in. What you can do to catch them happening early is to regularly monitor the evaluation outcomes.

Monitoring will review any inconsistencies and help you identify potential bias. It might also reveal ways you can improve your pay-for-performance process so you get more accurate assessments from now on. The following table shows the key metrics you should track.

Metric	Why It Matters
Pay increases by gender/race.	This will be part of your equity audit. By following it, you can identify any patterns of inequity in merit-based raises.
Bonus amounts by role and demographic	This is another metric you can track with your equity audits. Use it to find disparities in reward distributions.
Performance ratings by team/manager	This metric will reveal leniency/severity bias in evaluation practices.
Eligibility and participation in programs	Track to be sure all employees are made aware of training or other programs to improve their performance. Not only will this expose the groups who are consistently ignored for those opportunities, but it will show you where you can improve your offerings to help everyone have equal access to performance pay.
Employee perception of fairness	These surveys are integral for discovering potential bias in your organization as they measure how much your employees trust you and are satisfied with your pay-for-performance system.

RESPONDING TO WHAT YOU FIND

Of course, monitoring anything doesn't create change. You have to use the data to identify the gaps so you can create a resolution to eliminate them.

Here's how to examine your gaps:

- **Investigate the root causes.** How or when did this issue originate? Was it in goal setting, in evaluating, or in reward distribution?

- **Adjust criteria or processes.** This might mean revisiting the objectivity concept to more specifically clarify expectations or to dial in your metrics.
- **Communicate openly.** Use your monitoring efforts as another avenue to be transparent by letting employees know what you're monitoring and how you intend to use it to improve your pay-for-performance system.

Monitoring will prove itself to be a method for continuous improvement. Being transparent with the results and how you're using the data will support and prove your commitment to equity. So, while it might seem like one more step to take in an already long list of things to do, it will pay off for you.

ALIGNING PERFORMANCE WITH EQUITY

Sometimes I get pushback from companies that want to be equitable companies, but they fear that focusing on equity will mean they cannot focus on performance. Hopefully, I've eliminated that fear with this chapter, because performance and equity do not have to be competing priorities. In fact, they can support each other to the greater benefit of the organizations. Being equitable with your pay-for-performance programs can lead to higher engagement, retention, and performance.

CLOSING THE WAGE GAP FOR GOOD

By now, you know what to do to identify any potential pay disparities in your organization, how to remediate them, and how to maintain pay equity as part of your cyclical year. You understand the laws behind it, and you are prepared to coach your employees on this topic. Great! You have what it takes to be an equitable organization today. But what about tomorrow?

Few, if any, organizations are static. Most are intent on scaling, but even if you are in a healthy place and want to cruise there for a while, you'll still discover that your company will need to morph and evolve over time. Your workforce will expand and contract. Your state and federal governments frequently review and change employment laws. And there will be other situations that seem to pop out of nowhere (COVID-19) that can impact you in ways you never expected. Maintaining equity for the long haul requires a willingness to stay on top of things, pivot when appropriate, and have the tenacity to stay committed to the equity cause.

The good news is that it is easier with long-term strategies. In this last chapter, I'll talk about how organizations can evolve to sustain equity, how organizational transformation plays a role in that evolution, and how fair compensation is expected to change in the future.

LONG-TERM STRATEGIES FOR SUSTAINING PAY EQUITY

Sustaining pay equity requires the same three necessary protocols for maintaining any successful initiative in a business: making the systems or processes related to it repeatable, building in a mechanism for accountability, and having cultural reinforcement. When you nail those, the pay gaps you've been able to close will have a better chance of staying closed.

Let's look at how you can take action on each one of them.

MAKE PAY EQUITY AUDITS ROUTINE

This concept was brought up in Chapter 5, where, in step ten for conducting a pay equity audit, I spoke about planning for monitoring and conducting audits on a regular basis (annually or biannually) as a means of being proactive. Doing so will make you aware of potential disparity issues, so you can fix them before anyone has a chance to file a complaint against you, or your state attorney general sends a notice saying you're out of legal compliance.

For your recurring audits, you'll want to use the structured methodology of your first one and include all the compensation elements you originally considered: base pay, bonus pay, equity in the company, etc. The goal will be to review and analyze the data across gender, race, age, or whatever demographics you looked at before, and if anything triggers a closer look, review it and put an action plan into place. Rinse and repeat in six to twelve months.

Do the same audit all the time. But I'd like to encourage you to include a moment to pause beforehand for reflection. It's always possible that a new variable needs to be weighed and considered before completing the audit. Here are a few other things to think about:

- **System or policy changes.** If you found a disparity during an audit and instituted a policy change, system update, or some form of remediation, before doing the next audit, think about the impact you expected from that change. Will there be new data on this go-around that can confirm (or not) how successful you were? How can you find and analyze that data?

- **Legal compliance.** Check in with your state and federal laws to be sure nothing has changed in the interim. If you have remote employees in other states or countries, check for changes in their laws too.
- **Clean data.** Data can always get corrupted. Clean it before each audit. Don't assume that because it was clean the last time that it will be clean this time.
- **Company changes.** Have there been any structural changes in the organization? New departments? Collapsed or combined teams? More people working remotely? These things can impact audit results.
- **Job comparables.** Sometimes jobs that have substantially the same compensable factors drift into separate categories. Reviewing job descriptions will help you identify when comparing apples to apples shifts to comparing apples to oranges.

These regular audits won't just maintain your commitment to equity; they will help equity remain embedded in your culture over time, as it becomes a business norm, which is great. However, like everything else that is a business norm, you'll also need a means of holding people accountable for your fair practices.

ESTABLISH EQUITY GOVERNANCE

I spoke about establishing governance and oversight in Chapter 8 and am building on that here. In this chapter,

I'm placing greater emphasis on maintaining formalized accountability as your company grows and evolves in the future. Here are a few things to consider implementing:

- Establish a pay equity council or task force responsible for analyzing audit results and following up on remediations. Periodically change the individuals in this group. By keeping the same individuals on it year after year, you can unintentionally create a bias.
- Tie equity to performance expectations year after year. When it's time to evaluate leadership, including the executives, what are the KPIs you can attach to their expectations? Do they change from year to year? If so, update the scorecards or appraisals.
- Annually schedule time to review all compensation policies and systems. Are they still in alignment with your organization's commitment to equity? Do any new ones support your equity goals? Or do they run counter to them?

The idea behind creating governance strategies is to make equity something that holds multiple people accountable for it to succeed. The more people you have vested in maintaining equity as a corporate goal, the more it becomes central to how your company operates. When it becomes a core ingredient in your culture, you are less likely to find yourself behind the eight ball with pay disparities.

If equity is to become a permanent objective, which it should, that means you must make it a strategic priority, as I discussed in Chapter 8. Now it's time to look at ways you can "future-proof" your commitment to keeping it a priority.

The first place to look is in your communications. You should always make your equity efforts visible in your branding and recruitment messaging; it should never be a one-and-done concept. Ensure that from here on out, all your regular pay audits, promotions, and salary bands are updated and broadcast to prove your commitment to equity is here to stay.

When recruiting, always update your language so it remains inclusive. Remember, your best candidates will be those looking at their career options through a lens of "How can I grow in this company?" They'll interpret a job posting that speaks only of a required pedigree or experience as looking frozen in time. Instead, emphasize the skills needed for the job now, as well as the growth potential for the position in all postings.

For your current employees, particularly those in leadership positions, think about how you can prepare them for the future. Provide training opportunities where they can learn how to manage the impact on equity initiatives from things like company growth, mergers, restructuring, new laws, or other scenarios. Since almost no one gets a gold watch for fifty years in a company anymore, put some thought into succession frameworks. Inquire about safeguards for your initiatives should equity-minded managers or team leaders depart.

When I talk about management or leadership roles in equity, I mean everyone in a decision-making position for compensation. However, we know the brunt of this work falls into the hands of the HR team. To secure equity in the future, they will need to have performance expectations and goals set for them around tracking metrics related to representation in promotions, fairness in performance evaluations, and pay equity outcomes.

Additionally, while no one in your organization can be expected to have ESP, there should be someone staying abreast of predicted trends. Market shifts, ever-evolving legal compliance requirements, and even the diversity of your workforce will create the need for your compensation strategies to change. Usually, these changes do not occur unexpectedly, but people can identify, track, and plan for them.

All these long-term strategies will support you as your organization faces a changing environment and outside influences. But sometimes changes come from within. Let's look at how equity fits into organizational transformation.

INTEGRATING EQUITY INTO ORGANIZATIONAL TRANSFORMATION

Any mergers, scaling, downsizing, and other forms of corporate transformations will cause you to adapt your equity measures so they remain valid for the organization. Often, the evidence of companies evolving is first seen at the ground level: in the jobs of the employees. That's why job descriptions must be reviewed on a regular basis and reevaluated to make sure they remain market competitive. Similarly, organizational charts need to change as hierarchies get redefined. These shifts will impact your audits as well as your strategies to maintain equity.

Here's how you can keep your equitable company ready to face those situations in the future:

- Regularly reevaluate the methods used to access and group jobs.
- Be open to nonlinear career paths and nontraditional credentials—meaning, ask yourself, does someone need a particular degree if they have a successful track record that proves they can do the job? Do they need to have experience in a specific industry if their job responsibilities were identical in a different one?
- Make sure to always include emerging, remote, and hybrid roles in pay equity analyses.

In short, we need to review how the work is structured, not

how the jobs are paid, to maintain equity. Of course, that doesn't prevent looking at compensation as your organization undergoes change.

COMPENSATION AND THE EVOLVING WORKPLACE

I almost began this section with, "We are entering a new era of work," but isn't that always where we are—about to enter one era or another? The world is constantly changing, and our businesses must evolve if we are to keep or grow our market share. This means your compensation models will always face tests, and they will need to be flexible and adaptable. However, they will always need to be transparent.

Transparency is not a trend; it's a permanent expectation: Employees expect visibility into how their pay is determined. They will always want to work for employers who are honest. And they will always want to be compensated in a way that meets their needs and that grows with them.

To continue providing fair compensation for your employees, you must plan for their future as you plan for your company's future. That means:

- We must review and adapt benefit packages. Do you have a pension? Probably not. Are 401(k)s here to stay?

Maybe. Will something else be created to replace them? Another maybe. Are you ready to offer the next thing? Likewise, health insurance is in a perpetual state of transformation, and who would have expected pet insurance to be a competitive benefit? Look forward and be open to updating your benefits package.

- Do not finalize Incentive and recognition programs. As job descriptions evolve and grow over time, so too should bonuses and recognition.
- Nontraditional pay models, like gig and fractional work, are broadening their reach and finding their way into ever more industries and markets. How can your company prepare to be fair and equitable to the people you hire in those positions?

What I hope I've been able to emphasize with the previous bullet points (and throughout the book) is that not only is maintaining equity a continuous process, but it also affects everyone in your organization. That doesn't mean creating equity sets you up so you pay everyone the same; it means you give your employees what they need to thrive in their positions now and into the future.

THE FUTURE

The future of compensation will require equity to be embedded in all your systems, processes, and policies. And you must create all of them to adapt and improve over time. You will achieve this by leveraging your ongoing data monitoring and AI-driven insights to flag inequities, hopefully before they occur, proactively remedying them, and developing leadership with equity in mind. Going back to the idea of intention, all the above are intentional actions.

We must always remember that pay equity is possible, but only if we choose to pursue it with intention. Whether you're a CEO, an HR leader, a compensation analyst, or an employee, you have a role to play in sustaining an equitable culture in your organization. You must be willing to:

- Ask questions about salary decisions and compensation philosophies.
- Demand transparency regarding who the decision-makers are. How do they make decisions, and what are the factors in those decisions?
- Challenge your assumptions. Just because "this is how we've always done it" doesn't work anymore. There must be a willingness to explore new ideas, new philosophies, and new strategies.
- Back up values with action—walk the equity talk.

We did not create the wage gap overnight, and we will not eliminate it overnight. But with bold leadership, inclusive systems, and empowered people, we can close it for good.

The future of work is equitable. Let's build it together.

CONCLUSION

WHY PAY EQUITY IS EVERYONE'S RESPONSIBILITY

Let's go back to the story I told you about at the beginning of the book, when I had all those managers approaching me in great concern. After watching my presentation, they knew they had a pay equity problem but didn't know how to handle it. After they disclosed to me what was happening, I had to report it to the head of their HR. So, I scheduled a meeting with them, and together we developed an action plan—one that aligns with the steps outlined in this book.

The HR head didn't flinch at the concept of doing the analysis. In fact, once they learned about the pay disparities, they wanted to jump in right away and start making things right. But revelation of the disparity's true size caused hesitation, *not* due to a desire to abandon their people. The magnitude of the problem concerned them.

The company is enormous, and about 15,000 employees were not being paid equitably. The CEO and the HR leader were absolutely terrified that getting everyone paid at the levels they needed to be would cost millions they hadn't budgeted for.

That wasn't the first time I'd ever received such pushback. Thankfully, I've enough experience in this realm to know that it's seldom (if ever) the case. In fact, one of the largest companies I've worked with has a multimillion-dollar payroll. Their total spend on equity adjustments? About $250,000. That's it.

Yes, those are increases that get compounded annually, so from a CFO's perspective, they're a "forever expense" for as long as that employee remains. But even then, it's not the massive financial burden people imagine it to be. CEOs and CFOs often fear they're staring down millions in corrections. In reality, it never plays out that way, and besides, no one wants to be the company that doesn't pay fairly.

And here's something I always recommend: prioritize. You don't have to fix everything overnight. Most pay equity laws allow you to make corrections over a reasonable period. That gives you a chance to be strategic and focus on the most urgent gaps first before working through the rest in a phased, thoughtful way.

I explained all that to the company, but they decided to just bite the bullet, make every adjustment necessary, and get everyone paid a fair wage. They did right by their people, and that one act, compounded by their transparency about it, created a ripple effect that reached across the entire organization. Their employees appreciated the pay increases, and everyone's trust and commitment to the organization strengthened.

I love telling their story because it's a great example of a gratifying moment when everything we advocate for plays out the way it should.

I still work with that company today, and they remain in excellent shape for equity and compensation practices. That all started in 2018, and they've stayed committed ever since.

In the end, it's not just about compliance. It's about integrity. When organizations choose to act from that place, good things happen. I've seen it firsthand.

WHAT WE'VE LEARNED

I guess one moral of the story is, if they can do it, so can you. Now that you've finished this book, you have the guidance and framework you need to do it.

The first step is to acknowledge that you might have a pay disparity problem and be willing to confirm whether you do. Again, no one wants to think they're the person who would pay someone unfairly. But it happens.

Once you look under your compensation hood, familiarize yourself with the federal and state laws that apply to your organization. Don't forget to review the laws in other states or countries if you have employees working remotely.

When you're ready to begin the audit, start by creating fair pay within the company, then work on comparing salaries to the market. After benchmarking your positions, you'll create a strategy to balance your internal equity with what the market is paying. Only then will you be prepared to do the ten-step pay equity audit. The audit will reveal your pay gaps, which will determine the organizational strategies you need to use to close them.

Throughout the process, you'll grow more comfortable being transparent about your pay equity matters. That'll help embed equity into your organizational culture, which will be one way you maintain equity. Other ways to maintain it are by making audits a repeatable activity, using pay-for-performance strategies built around equity, educating your workforce, and empowering them to self-advocate. Then, future proofing the equity in your company will be a matter of building on what you did to create it and keeping everyone mindful of it and committed to it.

A SHARED COMMITMENT

Yes, equity is a shared commitment. Whether you are reading this as a business leader, an HR professional, a compensation expert, or an employee trying to understand your own worth, your role matters. Becoming an equitable company is like every other attempt to sustain positive change. It comes from a collective willingness to question how well you are doing, analyze the answers you discover, and then take action on remedying the situation.

Here's how each of us can contribute to making pay equity a reality:

- If you're a leader, model the behaviors you want to see in everyone else within your organization. Be open and willing to talk about pay matters whenever someone asks about it. Make equity a priority by incorporating it into your business strategy, decision-making processes, and goal setting. Remember to always be transparent about your equity status, your progress, and even your missteps along the way.
- If you're an HR or compensation professional, most likely you'll be the one who is the architect and general

contractor for building the systems required for making fairness possible. Make sure those systems are operational and repeatable, and the pay structures you create are resilient, flexible, and bias-resistant. You'll probably also lead the effort to hold people accountable for misusing equity systems or ignoring policies. Be prepared for that by having measures in place that you'll hope to never use.

- If you're an employee, always remember you may have more power than you realize. Know your rights, ask questions, get involved with your employee groups, and use your voice to push for transparency and justice. Let your curiosity spark conversations around wages and be insistent about fairness.

I hope this text conveys that equity's pursuit is not the end, but its preservation is. That requires persistence, discipline, and a willingness of everyone in the company to show up and demand it. It's a matter of intentional action taken by everyone in the organization, which includes you, the person reading this book.

Your organization will develop, and the work world will develop, but being equitable will always be a defining characteristic to set you apart in the market. Embrace your part in maintaining it, and let this book be the beginning of your action plan, not the end of your equity journey.

WHERE DO WE GO NOW?

Our relationship doesn't have to end here. I'd love to continue being a resource for you. At my organization, Compensation and HR Group (CHRG), we're a team of experienced compensation and HR professionals committed to helping organizations like yours thrive.

We work alongside you to align your people strategies with your business goals, which of course include completing equity audits and creating remediation plans. But we don't stop there. You can reach out to us for a full range of consulting services—from strategic planning and program design to implementation and evaluation. Our support also includes comprehensive training, market research, and data-driven analysis to inform your decisions.

Guided by our core values of respect, integrity, and excellence, we take the time to understand your organization's unique culture and needs. This allows us to develop compensation and HR programs that are not only effective but tailored to your goals.

Whether you're looking to recruit, pay, reward, or keep top talent, my team and I are here to help. If you need compensation consulting or training for yourself or your managers, we're ready to support you with the tools and insights featured throughout this book.

Feel free to reach out at dweaver@comphrgroup.com, connect with me on LinkedIn at linkedin.com/in/davidkweaver, or follow me on X @DavidWeaverCOMP.

ABOUT THE AUTHOR

DAVID WEAVER is an award-winning author of the bestselling business book *Pay Matters: The Art and Science of Employee Compensation* and the children's book *Pay Matters to Kids*. He is the founder of the Compensation and HR Group, an instructor at the Compensation Analyst Academy, and the executive director of the Pay Matters Foundation, which is an independent and private nonprofit organization dedicated to providing people with knowledge about pay.